SALES

BAD

ASS

ERY

SALES

Kick ass.

BAD

Take Names.

ASS

Crush the Competition.

ERY

FRANK J. RUMBAUSKAS

WILEY

For general information on our other products and services or for technical support, please contact our Customer Care Department within the United States at (800) 762–2974, outside the United States at (317) 572–3993 or fax (317) 572–4002.

Wiley publishes in a variety of print and electronic formats and by print-on-demand. Some material included with standard print versions of this book may not be included in e-books or in print-on-demand. If this book refers to media such as a CD or DVD that is not included in the version you purchased, you may download this material at http://booksupport.wiley.com. For more information about Wiley products, visit www.wiley.com.

Library of Congress Cataloging-in-Publication Data:
Names: Rumbauskas, Frank J., 1973-2018 author.

Title: Sales badassery : kick ass, take names, crush the competition. / Frank J. Rumbauskas, Jr.
Description: First Edition. | Hoboken : Wiley, 2019. | Includes index. | Identifiers: LCCN 2018051261 (print) | LCCN 2019003426 (ebook) | ISBN 9781119546351 (AdobePDF) | ISBN 9781119546375 (ePub) | ISBN 9781119546344 (hardback)
Subjects: LCSH: Sellling. | Marketing. | BISAC: BUSINESS & ECONOMICS / Motivational. | BUSINESS & ECONOMICS / Marketing / Direct.
Classification: LCC HF5438.25 (ebook) | LCC HF5438.25 .R856 2019 (print) | DDC 381–dc23

LC record available at https://lccn.loc.gov/2018051261
Printed in the United States of America

V10008557 030519

Dedicated to Agnes and Maeve, whom I love more than anything else in this world. And to my wonderful grandmother, "Nannie Bea," who has always been like a mother to me. I wouldn't be who I am today without her and her unlimited, unconditional love and encouragement.

CONTENTS

PREFACE

"What's your excuse, scumbag?"

—Gunny Sargent Hartman, *Full Metal Jacket*

Imagine it's your third meeting with a prospect whom some might call a "whale"—sales lingo for a prize prospect who can potentially put a lot of money in your pocket.

You ask for the order, and the objections come flying out of the prospect's mouth. You wonder if they're real or just excuses. Unfortunately, you have no way of knowing. (Yet.)

After handling them as best you can, you ask for the sale again, and during the 20 seconds of silence that feels like 20 hours, your palms are sweaty, your heart is racing, and you're secretly terrified of hearing the word *no*.

Finally, the silence is broken: The prospect said no. Your fear came true.

You thank the person for their time, put the paperwork back in your briefcase, and head back to the office to make your cold calls for the day and hopefully "drum up some business." You put on a happy face as you're leaving but inside you're devastated and feel like a failure. You even feel contempt for that prospect.

Perhaps its contempt for *yourself* you're feeling.

When you return, your sales manager asks if you got the deal or not. Lacking the courage to say no, you say that they're very interested but they're not ready yet and you'll get the deal in a few months. Back at your desk you simply move them to a later date on your sales forecast.

WHAT'S WRONG WITH THIS PICTURE?

What's wrong is that you had no power, no balls, and never had any to begin with. If you did, you'd have gotten the sale. You're lacking in self-confidence, and you treat prospects as superiors. You beg, chase, and otherwise supplicate to them. You see them the same way as you see your boss: as the person in charge. You even lied to your sales manager to keep his or her approval.

Now reverse the situation:

It's only your second appointment, not third, and you confidently ask for the order. You sit back in your chair perfectly calm and quietly excited to close this sale.

The prospect knows from past experience that you won't tolerate any nonsense so that strategy is avoided; however, he throws out a couple of token objections, but you know they're not true; after all, you've been trained on how to detect lies. You ask for the order again. You're relaxed, and the 20 seconds that pass actually feel like only 20 seconds.

The prospect says yes, signs the contract, and submits the request for the check.

He trusts you, likes you, loves the fact that you're a no-B.S. kind of person who doesn't take any shit from anyone, and is excited to start this new business relationship.

In fact, you've been so beneficial, not only in providing an ideal solution to your new customer, but also in *guiding him to make a decision and say yes* that he's glad to simply know you as a business associate.

You thank each other as you leave and the prospect agrees to meet you for coffee or lunch soon just to "talk shop." He sees you as an equal and looks forward to meeting again. You plan on getting high-value referrals and introductions from him and, who knows, perhaps an invitation to a members-only business roundtable group. (Hint: If you can get into one of those, first make sure it's legit and not based on a national franchise, then … accept!)

You get back to the office and your sales manager, who depends on you to make his numbers while also fearing that you'll take his job one day, says, "So, did you get the deal?"

He asks with a smirk on his face because he knows damn well that you did.

Your co-workers assume the manager just hands you these deals because you make sales look so effortless.

That's because you're not a loser. *You're a Sales Badass.*

Sound too good to be true? Don't worry, because it's not, and it won't take a huge amount of effort or time to become one. I'm not going to ask you to say certain affirmations daily or do a silly morning routine or any woo-woo crap like that.

Since I'm the original Sales Badass, there's no bullshit or fluff in this book. It gets right down to business.

THE PROBLEM WITH MODERN SALES PROFESSIONALS

Life is more stressful than ever, and many experts on the topic believe that our bodies and brains haven't evolved to handle this level of stress and distractions yet, because it wasn't much more than a hundred years ago that life was extremely simple.* Now we have smartphones, traffic, email to get to, planes to catch, and life is a hundred times more fast-paced than it was yesteryear.

---

* In all fairness, they did have lawyers and politicians back then, so …

In other words, life is already stressful enough, without throwing a challenging sales quota and modern living expenses on top of it—let alone a barking sales manager.

That's why the vast majority of sales reps are losers who usually keep track of job openings in case they get fired. Instead of using LinkedIn to generate new business, they use it to have Plan B jobs to fall back on. And anyone who places the fear of being fired and needing a new job above the importance of generating new business is a loser. Plain and simple.

Am I politically correct? No. Do I tell the truth? Yes, and most people can't handle the truth, which is precisely why they invented political correctness in the first place.

As candidate Donald Trump said in a debate, "Frankly, I don't have time for political correctness, and I don't think this country has time for political correctness."

I'm telling *you,* right now, that *you* do not have time for political correctness, so grab your balls and just deal with it. Life will always be hard if you're not willing to do the hard work—and accept the truth—to change that.

How many times have you heard salespeople say things like, "I'll be at your beck and call if you become my customer," or, "I'm willing to do whatever it takes to earn your business," or, "I'll even give you my home number so you can reach me anytime there's an issue."

Please, someone hand me a barf bag. That kind of weakness makes me want to puke. And you can be certain that I never, ever buy from people like that, nor did I ever once give away my home phone number during my sales career! My home is *my* castle—not that of my customers.

Worst of all, saying and doing things like that gives 100% of your power over to the prospect, massively hurting your chances of closing a deal and guaranteeing that you'll continue to struggle to make sales and have prospects walk all over you, at least for as long as you can hang onto your sales job.

Meanwhile, a small percentage of sales professionals are winners. They make selling look effortless. They have an extremely high closing rate. They know when someone is lying. They're mildly intimidating yet very likable and easy to trust—hallmarks of any great negotiator. They have advanced sales skills that others do not, because *they took the time to learn them and practice them.* They're always the best-dressed person in the room, even in casual clothes.

If I could wear dark three-piece suits in 115-degree Phoenix weather, then what the hell is *your* excuse for not dressing to the nines? (Readers in the Middle East shall be exempt from this particular rule!) At least here in Dallas our 100° summer days are not accepted as excuses to dress like slobs.

(Definition of slob: Anyone considering themselves a "sales professional" who is wearing anything less than full-blown business attire. Golf shirts and khakis are not business attire—they're golf attire, and we all know that "I close deals on the golf course!" really translates into "I trick my boss into paying for my golf rounds and the dumbass actually thinks I'm hosting prospects.")

Most importantly of all, the Sales Badass will never ever take any shit from anyone. It's not about being a jerk, it's simply a mindset of tolerating zero nonsense from others. Because nonsense = negativity, and the fastest shortcut to success is to eliminate negativity from your mind and your life.

These are the people I call Sales Badasses. It's not something they're born with. Believe me, I was the biggest loser wimp my first few years in sales. I cold called, I begged, I pleaded ... but at least I didn't whine about how much my monthly bills were, like one particular loser of a sales manager used to tell us! Yeah, like Barry's monthly expenses really motivated *me* to sell something ...

You can, and will, learn Sales Badassery in this book. Once you do, you'll find that sales just happen—people simply buy—when you're in front of a qualified prospect with a current need for what you sell.

A MODERN-DAY WARRIOR

Imagine your job title has nothing to do with sales and your business cards show your position as a "Modern-Day Warrior."

How would you feel? Would you ever be nervous walking into a sales appointment, or taking a call from an irate customer?

No, you wouldn't. You'd feel strong and powerful. Most of all, you'd feel ready. You mind is prepared for anything that comes your way. You're ambitious. You know where you're going in life. You understand that setbacks and disappointments are merely ways to grow through struggle, or "gain from pain." You're an honest person with integrity. You never, ever seek the approval of others. Ever.

As Napoleon Hill once wrote, nature plants the seeds of discontent in all of us, which compels us to "Keep Up with the Joneses" and put on a good showing and finally be forced to experience *growth through struggle.*

A good friend officiated my wedding, and he wrote the vows and kept them secret, as a surprise for us. We were nervous! In the end, we loved them, and since my friend knows I'm a huge Rush fan, one of my vows was:

"To be a modern-day warrior with a mean, mean stride."

And that's what you're going to be very soon: A modern-day warrior with a mean, mean stride.

And I mean that literally—you'll learn the importance of how you walk in the body language chapter!

Do you ever look forward to the weekend and love Fridays? Do you dread going to work on Monday? Do you hit your snooze button multiple times and just don't want to get up for work?

When you're in the office, do you keep checking your watch, waiting for five o'clock to come? If so, you're not a modern-day warrior yet, but that will begin to change, starting right now.

THE MAN WITHOUT A SMILE

Many people comment that I should smile in my headshot photos. In reality, I generally do smile, and especially so when meeting someone for the first time, in a very specific way that you're going to learn.

Q: Why don't I smile on my headshot and business card photos?

A: First, because everyone else does, and second, because many wildly successful and powerful people don't.

I got the idea from Donald Trump who, whether you love him, hate him, or are indifferent as I am, almost never smiles in photos, In fact, his original presidential photo had a downright angry face on it! Why? To put America's enemies on notice that there's a new sheriff in town. (In other words, to convey power.) Eventually he caved and replaced it with a smile on his face, but only after he succeeded in life and then achieved the ultimate success, being elected president.

Notice also how he avoided phony smiles at all the debates in 2016. You may have also noticed that he always had his suit jacket unbuttoned while all the others were buttoned up. Again, this achieves differentiation, and you'll learn later on about why it makes people unconsciously like and trust you.

Dan Kennedy is another—unless you see a photo of him on stage speaking, he never smiles in his headshots. And he is the all-time King of direct response marketing. Not bad, eh?

Most importantly, a serious look implies power. That's why, every time a real estate agent asks me for sales advice, I tell them to replace the smiling photo with a serious look, or better yet, to just get rid of the damned thing altogether.

Not a single one has followed that advice.

It's too bad, because if any one of them did it, that person would have differentiation. And with differentiation comes a faster and easier path to power.

And finally, with a serious look in your photos, you'll be taken more seriously by others.

SELLING VERSUS NEGOTIATING: THE IMPORTANCE OF POWER

Every sales interaction is a negotiation. Even the very first contact, whether it's a cold call or otherwise, is a negotiation; the salesperson is negotiating with the prospect to get a meeting, while the prospect is trying to get the sales rep off the phone. We usually tend to think of negotiating in the form of price haggling, yet all of selling is negotiation, whether it's trying to get an appointment, trying to close a sale, trying to agree on a price—you name it.

Here's why having power in sales is so important: In every negotiation, the person who shows up with the power, who grabs it at the beginning and keeps it through to the end, will win. It's really that simple.

Now think about a typical sales appointment. It's obviously a negotiation, because the salesperson wants a sale at a good price and nice commission, while the prospect either wants to get rid of the salesperson or wants an absurdly steep discount.

Guess who will win in that meeting? That's right—the person with power.

The key is to show up as a powerful person, to seize the power at the very beginning of the sales process, and keep it through to the very end. And by the very end, I mean just that; once you've closed a sale, you'll want to build and maintain a relationship with that new customer, which will then lead to referrals and introductions, which are the best leads on the planet.

To put it very simply, the person who needs something loses, and the other person wins.

That's why I've written books and courses on why you should never, ever cold call.

Anyone who makes a cold call is subcommunicating to the other person that he wants or needs a sale. The specific action of making a cold call automatically gives away all of your power to the prospect.

Now reverse the situation: Let's say you've read my other books and know how to get prospects to come to you through a well-organized self-marketing plan.

What happens then?

That's right, the prospect is subcommunicating a need. That means they handed all their power over to you. In that situation, you'll get the sale every time and you'll get it at full price.

LET'S KICK SOME ASS

The bottom line is that power is everything in sales, so let's get started. It's time to drop your old ways of selling and transform you into a Sales Badass.

Welcome to the world of Sales Badassery!

Frank J. Rumbauskas

SALES

BAD

ASS

ERY

1

SALES BADASSES ARE INSTANTLY LIKEABLE

The Secrets of Making People Like and Trust You Instantly—and Making Them Buy

Sales Badass. Just the name conjures up images of some Hollywood-type sales pro with slicked back hair, an $8,000 custom suit, an imposing figure with a serious look and strong body language. Someone like Alec Baldwin's character in the movie *Glengarry, Glen Ross*.

It hardly conjures up images of someone who is instantly likeable; however, one of the primary skills of the Sales Badass is to do just that—be not only likeable to prospects, but also to gain instant likeability and immediate trust that is enduring. It will not only set the ball rolling in motion to get the sale with no trouble from competitors, it will stick all the way through that sales pro's relationship with the prospect, soon to be customer.

Politicians are prime examples of likeable bad asses—they can be dishonest, deceptive, and downright ruthless. Donald Trump is by far one of the most polarizing presidents of all time, and yet those who have met with him, in either a business or political context, will say he is the kindest and most gracious host who has ever had them.

Likewise, George W. Bush simply doesn't have a personality that the media likes. He just doesn't, and his frequently awkward speech comes across badly on television and leaves people with the impression that he's arrogant. As someone who lives just a couple of stoplights away and has talked with him numerous times, I can tell you he's the kindest, most generous man, who never speaks a bad word about anyone. I've never met Bill Clinton but have heard the same. (I met George H.W. Bush and it was true about him as well.)

Now consider people like me. It's true that I'm not exactly "Guy Smiley" … but it works. (However, smiling is extremely important in the right situations, as you'll learn in just a minute.) There are multiple reasons, but for now, let's start getting people to like you the moment they meet you. Keep in mind this doesn't just apply to sales—these are life skills that can be applied to any person-to-person interaction, so use them to your advantage whenever possible.

Here's a real-life example of how I used the strategy you're about to learn back in my days of advertising sales to win over a difficult yet valuable prospect everyone else in the office failed to engage. He was a big man from North Carolina, older and very, very Southern, and all the sales reps who failed to get through to him were kicked out of his office within a few minutes with a loud, Southern, "WE CAN'T DO BUSINESS! GET OUT!"

It's the kind of challenge I just couldn't resist, so I called and he accepted a meeting. (Note that he always accepted meetings, they just rarely lasted long.)

I arrived at his office and the receptionist asked me to take a seat while she notified him.

When it was time to go in, here's how I made my entrance, and notice precisely what I did:

First, I opened his office door and stopped in the door frame. Immediately upon making eye contact I flashed my eyebrows for a split-second, gave a broad smile that was complete and included my eyes and crow's feet, and tilted my head to the side. Since I was a man communicating with another man, the only time this technique is used, I also quickly jutted my chin out as well.

He welcomed me in with an equally huge smile, gave me a hearty handshake with both hands—always a good sign!—and invited me to sit down.

I maintained my likeability strategy through the appointment, changing facial expressions and smiling and not smiling when appropriate, using the head tilt when it made sense to do so, and I walked out with a deal without hearing, "WE CAN'T DO BUSINESS!"

Please note that the Sales Badassery Likeability Strategy includes three specific techniques. When I opened his office door and paused in the door frame until he made eye contact, that was a separate body language move that communicates dominance and so-called Alpha-ness. In other words, it set me up as a potential leader of the situation, which is how I ended up.

Now, before going any further, I need to eat some of my own words here. In the past I've always talked about the fact that you have to get your prospects to respect you in order to get a sale, and that being liked wasn't necessary. And it's true, to a degree. I've had plenty of customers who didn't necessarily like me; however, they all respected me, and it's why they bought from me in the first place. And they continued buying. I've always been critical of so-called "sales experts" who endlessly preach that you must be likeable to get lots of sales. I'm living proof that isn't true, but after adding likeability to the mix while *keeping* respectability, I've discovered a truly killer combination that will nail down the sale for you every time.

Just being likeable will get you sales—to a degree. Likewise, only getting respect from prospects will also get you sales—to a greater degree than likeability alone, but the one-two punch of both like and respect put together is really a knockout combination.

Before I go into the details of the Sales Badassery Likeability Strategy, know that this information was developed by the FBI's behavioral analysis experts and is routinely used by FBI agents who interrogate suspects, frequently with the suspect even saying, "Hey, for an FBI [interrogator/polygraph examiner/special agent], you're a pretty nice guy!"

THE THREE-STEP STRATEGY TO INSTANT LIKEABILITY

Remember those former US presidents I mentioned? Seemingly everyone who meets one will tell you that they "make you feel like the only person in the room." Having met three—Gerald Ford was the other, in case you're curious—I've not experienced that; however, as an expert on this topic, what I *have* noticed is what I'm about to explain in detail, and it's this sequence of techniques that creates the "only person in the room" feeling. (Something tells me that Bill Clinton only runs this on attractive women, but hey, who am I to judge?)

There are three steps you must execute immediately upon meeting someone new (four for men), sales prospect or otherwise, to get instant likeability and immediate yet lasting trust:

1. The eye flash
2. The full smile
3. The head tilt
4. The chin jut (for men only)

These are the so-called friend signals that our brains have developed to look for and recognize, all unconsciously. When someone meets you with a quick eye flash followed by a broad smile and head tilt, your logical brain doesn't say, "Wow, he did the eye flash and is now smiling with his head tilted. I guess I must like this person!" In fact, it all happens automatically and unconsciously.

If you've ever had a hunch that you didn't like someone, and who hasn't, it's likely because that person didn't send you the friend signals upon meeting. And when you meet someone, speaking in a professional sense, and notice there's just something about him or her that you like and you want to do business with that person, that's why. They unconsciously sent you the friend signals, your brain unconsciously interpreted them, and neither of you was ever aware of any of this going on.

The Eye Flash

We'll cover the eye flash first, followed by the other two, and then learn how to put them all together into one fluid action.

You're probably never even noticed it, but when you meet someone you like, you flash your eyebrows for just a split second; the actual time for a natural eyebrow flash is about one-sixth of one second, so yes, this will take practice to get it right!

Start observing other people when they meet you, even just walking down the street making eye contact and saying hello. The ones who respond positively to you will also unconsciously flash their eyebrows for about one-sixth of a second. (Of course, this doesn't work in New York City, where saying hi to random strangers will just make people assume you are insane, but it works great here in Dallas.)

Not only do our brains interpret this signal, they actually look for it! So, if the signal is present, what the other person's brain interprets is that we are not a threat, we are not dangerous and do not need to be avoided.

The eyebrow flash works exceptionally well at networking functions. Let's say you're at a large networking mixer in a big venue. Or even in a small one. Simply look for someone you'd like to talk to—it can be any person at random just to test this out—and send an eyebrow flash upon making eye contact.

If the person is interested in talking with you, you'll receive an eye flash right back. That's your green light to go introduce yourself and start a conversation. (And yes, this works in the dating game just as well as in the game of business.)

If you receive no eyebrow flash back—and you have to watch for it, because it's quick—you'll know not to waste time with that person. It could be a fluke and if it's an important person you can still try, assuming you use these techniques, but chances are it's not a good contact. (See, you're learning more of my signature "qualifying out" strategies without us even talking about qualifying prospects yet!)

On that same note, whether you're at a networking event looking for new contacts and prospects or a single person looking for a date, you can keep a keen eye for other people's eyebrow flashes and save a lot of wasted time avoiding the people who don't reciprocate yours.

Keep in mind that an effective, friendly eyebrow flash must be accompanied by brief eye contact. The human brain interprets extended eye contact from a stranger as a threat, at least speaking in terms of business relationships—this isn't a dating or flirting book. If you don't believe me, try it. You'll find that people are so put off by extended eye contact that they will go out of their way to avoid any further eye contact with you from that point on. And no, don't test this on high-value prospects or other contacts you'd like to make!

Most importantly, remember that it should last only one-sixth of a second. The first several times you try this you'll wind up doing an exaggerated eyebrow flash which other people will interpret as phony, and phoniness does not a solid relationship make. So take time to practice in front of a mirror, preferably daily for several days until you get this right. The key operational term here is brief—one-sixth of a second and that's it!

The Broad, Genuine Smile

For all my talk about looking serious in photos, a genuine smile is critical to gain trust and likeability from a prospect.

And I don't mean just any smile. No phony smiles here. No fake picture smiles here. (Don't you hate it when you've been holding a smile for what seems like forever and the person is still fiddling around with the camera? Yeah, me too. Just take the damn picture already.)

I mean a smile. A real smile. That means a smile that makes you look truly happy to meet someone. Indeed, it is the same smile that people show when they are genuinely happy!

The elements of the true smile are:

- A wide, broad smile
- A smile that extends and shows in your eyes
- A smile that's big enough to cause crow's feet (the little wrinkles outside your eyes when you are genuinely smiling) to appear

Again, you can practice all this in front of a mirror, and in fact you'll need to in order to ensure you have a genuine, effective smile; I know plenty of people who put on fake smiles and seem to force them. Even my conscious mind can detect phony smiles, let alone the unconscious part of my brain!

A smile is a powerful likeability signal. It puts people at ease, communicates friendliness and confidence, and makes you more attractive and desirable to do business with.

It also releases endorphins, the feel-good hormones in our brains that are most well known for the so-called runner's high or exercise high that many of us have experienced. They're also the body's natural painkillers and in fact attach to the same opioid receptors in the brain as actual opioid drugs, and as a result they make us feel more relaxed and at ease – which all just adds up to more self-confidence and ability to close the deal.

Perhaps most importantly, a genuine smile puts the *other* person at ease, makes them feel relaxed, and *it makes a person more receptive* to others or, in this case, *you*, dramatically increasing the odds that you'll close the sale.

Spend time practicing the real smile in the mirror. Unlike the eye flash, this one will be easy to perfect—just put on the kind of smile you experience when you are genuinely happy—seeing loved ones after a long time apart, seeing your kids at the end of the day, getting great news—you name it.

Beware of the fake or "forced" smile, which is instantly recognizable as fake, sometimes by the conscious mind, and always by the unconscious. The "real" smile is used with people we want to build a connection and relationship with, whether that happens to be personal or, in our case, business.

Once you've got that down, practice in a mirror with a correct split-second eyebrow flash immediately followed by a real smile. It did take me a little while to perfect this, so practice, practice, practice!

Now that you've got those two moves down, it's time for the easiest one.

The Head Tilt

The head tilt is the third component in the Sales Badassery Likeability Strategy and is the easiest to execute.

At the same time you put the broad, genuine smile on your face, you tilt your head to either side slightly. Which side doesn't matter unless the other person has their head tilted, in which case you want to mirror them and tilt in the same direction.

Don't make it overly exaggerated, either. Just a slight tilt to either side. You don't want to come across like you're doing it on purpose or trying too hard. That will effectively neutralize the entire likeability strategy.

Here's why the head tilt is such a powerful "like" indicator: Back in ancient times, or the time before writing, if you will, there were no guns and it was common practice, in battle or in murder, to sever an enemy's carotid artery, the large arteries on either side of the neck that feed the brain. Severing either carotid artery causes unconsciousness within seconds and death within minutes.

Because we're programmed to operate as we did back in the caveman days, thanks to evolution lagging by about a hundred thousand years, we still unconsciously guard our carotid arteries from anyone we don't trust.

For example, when we're with a person we don't know, don't trust, or have reason to believe is suspicious, we hold our heads perfectly upright. We don't realize we're doing this, we just do it. It's the same reason people tend to tense up their shoulders when under stress and drop them when relaxed; the uptight shoulders held high guard our carotid arteries from potential damage. Since our brains can't tell the difference between the stress of paying the bills or the stress of an enemy tribe member coming up from behind and slitting our throat, it's an automatic response to stress to tense up the shoulders and hold them higher than normal rather than letting them relax.

On the contrary, when we're around people we like, trust, know, and feel safe with, we naturally tilt our heads. We're okay with exposing our carotid arteries (or at least our brain is—remember this is all unconscious) in friendly company because there are no adversaries present wanting to slit our throats, keeping in mind our brains are still programmed for the caveman days.

That's why the head tilt is so effective in gaining likeability and trust from a prospect you're meeting for the very first time. Although they're not aware of it, their brains see our tilted heads and exposed arteries and tell them, "This person is okay—you can trust him or her and safely do business without getting burned."

It also subcommunicates to the prospect that you do not see that person as a threat. It mutually helps to identify two people to each other as "friendlies" rather than "adversaries" (see Figure 1.1). It sets the stage for a mutually beneficial sales transaction that will exclude your competition, or at least the ones who don't know this stuff, and you can still practice everything in this book and still remain a Sales Badass—just a very likeable, trustworthy Sales Badass!

For Men Only: The Chin Jut

Men reading this won't need an explanation—we all already notice that we tend to do a chin jut when we happen to run into a friend in public and want to make ourselves known.

FIGURE 1.1 President Ronald Reagan perfectly executing the broad smile, the head tilt, and the eye flash upon meeting Mikhail Gorbachev. If these techniques can topple the Soviet Union, what can they do for you?

This technique is best reserved for follow-up appointments or if you do indeed happen to run into your prospect in public. Giving the chin jut, which happens naturally along with the eyebrow flash (try it), identifies you as a friend, not just someone who is potentially friendly. It solidifies the bond between two men that was created upon the initial meeting.

Remember, this is a men-only technique. Women don't chin jut each other! So if you're a man, go to a mirror and do it. Notice how your eyebrows almost naturally flash when you do! And if they don't, then just keep practicing until you have it all put together in one smooth sequence: the eyebrow flash and chin jut simultaneously, immediately flowing smoothly into a genuine smile and head tilt.

Good news: You're in. And they like you already—before you've said a word!

Sales Badassery Truth

The Sales Badass always maintains an image of power—think Harvey Specter from the USA television show Suits—*however, the Sales Badass is always likeable and worthy of trust.*

2

SALES BADASSES NEVER DRESS LIKE SHIT

The Psychology of Good Clothes, and How to Use It

A VERY DISAPPOINTED PRINCESS

I'm not much of a *Star Wars* fan, but my wife and her brothers are huge fans, so I've had my share of exposure to it.

Remember the scene when Princess Leah had the skimpy bikini on, and Jabba the Hut came out with this ultrapowerful, uber-confident line, "Soon you will come to appreciate me"?

On top of his supreme confidence, he had wealth, power, servants … and yet Princess Leah was totally repulsed by him.

Why?

His appearance (and I have to assume his smell too, but that's another story).

I thought of this title chapter from the movie *Boiler Room*. It's that scene where Ben Affleck's character sits all the new recruits down in the conference room, sits down at the head of the table, and starts off the meeting with, "Most of you guys [pause] … dress like shit."

Then the camera shows the new recruits wearing cheap suits, bad ties, off-color shirts, and the like.

Here's the funny part: For years before that movie came out, I was the guy in the office dressed like Ben Affleck's character, and I constantly told everyone else in the office they all dressed like shit and needed to up their clothing game if they wanted to perform on my level. After all, they always asked what my secret was, when it was obvious that I looked like a CEO and they looked like someone from the mailroom by comparison.

They'd shoot right back with, "This golf shirt costs a hundred bucks" and yet I was the one racking up the biggest sales numbers in our entire region—and I was the only one in a suit during hot desert summers.

I had more than my share of heated arguments with fellow sales reps over this. I was frequently accused of getting freebie leads or call-ins from the company, which wasn't the case at all. We were on our own in terms of sales prospecting. And when I'd get one of those accusations, I'd shoot right back with, "Go out and buy a decent suit and wear it and you'll achieve the same."

In fact, there were several very talented sales professionals on the team; however, they all dressed overly casual in the hot desert summers and as a result they got crushed by competitors who show up looking like a CEO instead of a golf caddy.

The psychology of good clothes is absolute, and you cannot become a Sales Badass without dressing like a Sales Badass.

Let me repeat that: You *cannot* become a Sales Badass by dressing like everyone else, or worse, taking the very stupid but very typical loser sales trainer advice of "dress like your prospects to make them comfortable with you."

Let's use an example: Say you've been sued for a very large sum of money and it's critical that you find the best lawyer to represent you. You narrow your list after extensive research and show up at Attorney 1's office for an initial consultation and case review.

When the receptionist tells you to go in, the attorney is in jeans and a golf shirt.

What's your first impression? Do you think, "Wow, here's an impressive, imposing fellow who will own the other lawyer and the judge!" Or do you think, "Are you kidding me? *This* is Mr. Super-High-Power Lawyer? Give me a break!"

Remember, don't think of this in your regular context; think of it in the context of having been sued for everything you own. Even your house is at stake if you lose. Do you really want to hire Mr. Golf Shirt and Jeans to represent you?

You dismiss him and move on to Attorney 2.

Once admitted to his office, he stands to greet you, dressed impeccably in a finely tailored suit, colored shirt with a white collar, nice tie, and pocket square, cuff links, and of course, that million-dollar smile we discussed in the previous chapter, the kind that will win over a jury in a heartbeat.

Do you think, "Are you kidding me?" Or do you think, "Now this is what I'm talking about! He'll kick their ass!" You're not only eager to hire him, you're even willing to pay a higher retainer to him than you would have to Mr. Business Casual.

The same thought process and evaluation happens when a prospect meets you for the first time and sizes you up, either consciously or not.

If you don't stand head and shoulders above the crowd, they're going to think, "Ugh, another boring sales presentation with yet another boring sales rep." They'll literally expect a brutally boring Power Point presentation that puts the entire room to sleep.

If you're dressed to the nines—the way Ben Affleck ordered his employees to dress in *Boiler Room*, the prospect's thought process will be different. You're going to be seen, first and foremost, as someone with a high degree of attention to detail, something that's necessary for any salesperson with a reasonable expectation of properly serving their customers after the sale. It's the ones who do not have a high degree of attention to detail who screw things up, cause billing problems, missed delivery and installation dates, and the like.

Most of all, they'll see you as a winner. Why? Because it's the losers who dress like shit.

When I first formally learned about the psychology of good clothes, I'd already been practicing it for a long time. And I knew why I did so: Good clothes have *nothing* to do with impressing your prospect. At least not *that* much. However, they have *everything* to do with the impression they make on *you*!

By dressing above and beyond every other sales rep, and virtually all of my prospects for that matter, I not only gained a great deal of respect from others, but gained a tremendous amount of self-respect and self-confidence. Even now, if I have an important day or an important task to complete, despite the fact that I'll spend the day alone in my private office, I'll still dress to the nines for the effect it has on my own mind. The reactions from other people on the way to my office get me pumped up for the day and feeling like a billionaire. Regardless of whatever your current financial situation happens to be at the time, it not only makes you supremely self-confident, it also radiates that confidence so that others feed on it and want to know you and be your friend and do business with you.

Here's the thing about that old, time-worn "dress like your prospects" advice: It makes you equal to your prospect. However, people don't see those who are dressed equally as Badasses. To be a Sales Badass you must dress better than your prospects. The best way to gauge this is to dress like the people they turn to for advice.

Whom do people turn to for advice? Professionals such as attorneys, accountants, and the like. And I've already described the thought process of meeting a potential lawyer only to write the person off in your mind because they're not dressed to the expectations of that profession.

Likewise, if your manner of dress follows the "norm" of a modern sales professional, which sadly means khakis and golf shirts or dress shirts with no ties for men, and no jacket either, your prospects will be disappointed when they first set eyes on you.

They want to work with a true professional—so show up like a true professional and do not dress like shit!

My definition of dressing like shit when it comes to sales: anything that doesn't drop jaws and massively surpass your prospect's expectations.

But don't take my word for it. Remember when I said before I was "formally" introduced to the psychology of good clothes? That introduction came from the one and only Napoleon Hill, best known for his massive best-seller, *Think and Grow Rich.* I learned this from my favorite of his works, *The Law of Success,* first published in 1925 and subsequently in 1928. It's his magnum opus, about five times longer than *Think and Grow Rich,* and a book I refer to as the "Cliff Notes" version of that book.

Since the copyrights on that book have long expired and the work is now in the public domain, here it is right from Dr. Hill himself, excerpted from *The Law of Success*:

(NOTE: Because this true story occurred exactly 100 years ago from the time of this writing, I've included the modern-day dollar equivalents in brackets after each figure mentioned by Hill.)

The Psychology of Good Clothes

When the good news came from the theater of war, on November the eleventh, 1918, my worldly possessions amounted to but little more than they did the day I came into the world.
The war had destroyed my business and made it necessary for me to make a new start!
My wardrobe consisted of three well worn business suits and two uniforms which I no longer needed.

Knowing all too well that the world forms its first and most lasting impressions of a man by the clothes he wears, I lost no time in visiting my tailor.

Happily, my tailor had known me for many years, therefore he did not judge me entirely by the clothes I wore. If he had I would have been "sunk."

With less than a dollar in change in my pocket, I picked out the cloth for three of the most expensive suits I ever owned, and ordered that they be made up for me at once.

The three suits came to $375.00! [$11,000]

I shall never forget the remark made by the tailor as he took my measure. Glancing first at the three bolts of expensive cloth which I had selected, and then at me, he inquired:

"Dollar-a-year man, eh?"

"No," said I, "if I had been fortunate enough to get on the dollar-a-year payroll I might now have enough money to pay for these suits."

The tailor looked at me with surprise. I don't think he got the joke.

One of the suits was a beautiful dark gray; one was a dark blue; the other was a light blue with a pin stripe.

Fortunately, I was in good standing with my tailor, therefore he did not ask when I was going to pay for those expensive suits.

I knew that I could and would pay for them in due time, but could I have convinced him of that? This was the thought which was running through my mind, with hope against hope that the question would not be brought up.

I then visited my haberdasher, from whom I purchased three less expensive suits and a complete supply of the best shirts, collars, ties, hosiery and underwear that he carried.

My bill at the haberdasher's amounted to a little over $300.00. [$9,000]

With an air of prosperity I nonchalantly signed the charge ticket and tossed it back to the salesman, with instructions to deliver my purchase the following morning. The feeling of renewed self-reliance and success had begun to come over me, even before I had attired myself in my newly purchased outfit.

I was out of the war and $675.00 [$20,000]* in debt, all in less than twenty-four hours.

The following day the first of the three suits ordered from the haberdasher was delivered. I put it on at once, stuffed a new silk handkerchief in the outside pocket of my coat, shoved the $50.00 I had borrowed on my ring down into my pants pocket, and walked down Michigan Boulevard, in Chicago, feeling as rich as Rockefeller.

Every article of clothing I wore, from my underwear out, was of the very best. That it was not paid for was nobody's business except mine and my tailor's and my haberdasher's.

Every morning I dressed myself in an entirely new outfit, and walked down the same street, at precisely the same hour. That hour "happened" to be the time when a certain wealthy publisher usually walked down the same street, on his way to lunch.

I made it my business to speak to him each day, and occasionally I would stop for a minute's chat with him.

After this daily meeting had been going on for about a week I met this publisher one day, but decided I would see if he would let me get by without speaking.

---

* I personally own suits costing as much as $8,500 each so Hill's numbers, while seemingly high, are entirely realistic for such high-end clothes. Thankfully you don't need to spend that kind of money; I now buy suits at the Saks Fifth Avenue "Off Fifth" outlet stores when they have their frequent two-for-one sales, so I wind up paying around $300 per suit plus alterations. (And you can order online if you don't have a store locally.) It doesn't matter to me though. They look and feel just as good as the wicked expensive suits, plus I don't really worry about spilling coffee on them or anything like that, and as Hill said, they make me feel "as rich as Rockefeller"!

Watching him from under my eyelashes I looked straight ahead, and started to pass him when he stopped and motioned me over to the edge of the sidewalk, placed his hand on my shoulder, and said: "You look damned prosperous for a man who has just laid aside a uniform. Who makes your clothes?"

"Well," said I, "Wilkie & Sellery made this particular suit."

He then wanted to know what sort of business I was engaged in. That "airy" atmosphere of prosperity which I had been wearing, along with a new and different suit every day, had got the better of his curiosity. (I had hoped that it would.)

Flipping the ashes from my Havana perfecto, I said "Oh, I am preparing the copy for a new magazine that I am going to publish."

"A new magazine, eh?" he queried, "and what are you going to call it?" "It is to be named Hill's Golden Rule."

"Don't forget," said my publisher friend, "that I am in the business of printing and distributing magazines. Perhaps I can serve you, also."

That was the moment for which I had been waiting. I had that very moment, and almost the very spot of ground on which we stood, in mind when I was purchasing those new suits.

But, is it necessary to remind you, that conversation never would have taken place had this publisher observed me walking down that street from day to day, with a "whipped-dog" look on my face, an un-pressed suit on my back and a look of poverty in my eyes.

An appearance of prosperity attracts attention always, with no exceptions whatsoever. Moreover, a look of prosperity attracts "favorable attention," because the one dominating desire in every human heart is to be prosperous.

My publisher friend invited me to his club for lunch. Before the coffee and cigars had been served he had "talked me out of" the contract for printing and distributing my magazine. I had even "consented" to permit him to supply the capital, without any interest charge.

For the benefit of those who are not familiar with the publishing business may I now offer the information that considerable capital is required for launching a new nationally distributed magazine.

Capital, in such large amounts, is often hard to get, even with the best of security. The capital necessary for launching Hill's Golden Rule magazine, which you may have read, was well above $30,000.00 [$900,000], and every cent of it was raised on a "front" created mostly by good clothes. True, there may have been some ability back of those clothes, but many millions of men have ability who never have anything else, and who are never heard of outside of the limited community in which they live. This is a rather sad truth!

To some it may seem an unpardonable extravagance for one who was "broke" to have gone in debt for $675.00 worth of clothes, but the psychology back of that investment more than justified it.

The appearance of prosperity not only made a favorable impression on those to whom I had to look for favors, but of more importance still was the effect that proper attire HAD ON ME. I not only knew that correct clothes would impress others favorably, but I knew that good clothes would give me an atmosphere of self-reliance, without which I could not hope to regain my lost fortunes.

I got my first training in the psychology of good clothes from my friend Edwin C. Barnes, who is a close business associate of Thomas A. Edison. Barnes afforded considerable amusement for the Edison staff when he rode into West Orange on a freight train (not being able to raise sufficient money for the passenger fare) and announced at the Edison offices that he had come to enter into a partnership with Mr. Edison.

Nearly everyone around the Edison plant laughed at Barnes, except Edison himself. He saw something in the square jaw and determined face of young Barnes which most of the others did not see, despite the fact that the young man looked more like a tramp than he did a future partner of the greatest inventor on earth.

Barnes got his start, sweeping floors in the Edison offices!

That was all he sought—just a chance to get a toe-hold in the Edison organization. From there on he made history that is well worth emulation by other young men who wish to make places for themselves.

Barnes has now retired from active business, even though he is still a comparatively young man, and spends most of his time at his two beautiful homes in Bradentown, Florida, and Damariscotta, Maine. He is a multimillionaire, prosperous and happy. I first became acquainted with Barnes during the early days of his association with Edison, before he had "arrived."

In those days he had the largest and most expensive collection of clothes I had ever seen or heard of one man owning. His wardrobe consisted of thirty-one suits; one for each day of the month. He never wore the same suit two days in succession.

Moreover, all his suits were of the most expensive type. (Incidentally, his clothes were made by the same tailors who made those three suits for me.)

He wore socks which cost six dollars per pair.

His shirts and other wearing apparel cost in similar proportion. His cravats were specially made, at a cost of from five to seven dollars and a half each.

One day, in a spirit of fun, I asked him to save some of his old suits which he did not need, for me.

He informed me that he hadn't a single suit which he did not need!

He then gave me a lesson on the psychology of good clothes which is well worth remembering. "I do not wear thirty-one suits of clothes," said he, "entirely for the impression they make on other people; I do it mostly for the impression they have on me." Barnes then told me of the day when he presented himself at the Edison plant, for a position. He said he had to walk around the plant a dozen times before he worked up enough courage to announce himself, because he knew that he looked more like a tramp than he did a desirable employee.

Barnes is said to be the most able salesman ever connected with the great inventor of West Orange. His entire fortune was made through his ability as a salesman, but he has often said that he never could have accomplished the results which have made him both wealthy and famous had it not been for his under-standing of the psychology of good clothes.

I have met many salesmen in my time. During the past ten years I have personally trained and directed the efforts of more than 3,000 salespeople, both men and women, and I have ob-served that, without a single exception, the star producers were all people who understood and made good use of the psychol-ogy of clothes.

I have seen a few well dressed people who made no outstanding records as salesmen, but I have yet to see the first poorly dressed man who became a star producer in the field of selling.

I have studied the psychology of clothes for so long, and I have watched its effect on people in so many different walks of life, that I am fully convinced there is a close connection between clothes and success.

Take that story to heart as you power up your image and apply the psychology of good clothes to your own life. I have. The results will truly astound you.

Finally, although you always want to dress better than your prospects, don't overdo it, meaning calibrate it to your location and your industry. I remember someone from Montana explaining that "dressed to the nines" there means nice jeans, nice boots, and a nice shirt. No suits and no jackets. If you're in NYC or Dallas on the other hand, "dressed to the nines" means the way I look in recent photos. Like the one on this book.

Sales Badassery Truth

The Sales Badass never dresses equal or below the level of his prospects, but rather always dresses like the people they turn to for advice.

3

Sales Badasses Never Chase or Beg

Getting What You Want without Chasing, Begging, or Selling Your Soul

"I'll be at your beck and call if you become my customer."

"I'll do whatever it takes to earn your business."

"I'll even give you my home phone number, call anytime day or night if you need help after the sale."

How many times have you heard this kind of nonsense?

More specifically, how many times have *you* said things like this to try and close a sale?

That kind of talk is not the talk of a Sales Badass. That's talk for sales *losers*.

One of the key components of becoming a Sales Badass is never ever to beg, chase, or pursue prospects. You want them to pursue *you*.

A VERY SAD (AND BROKE) COLD CALLER

My very first sales job was in business-to-business telephone sales, or to put it simply, telemarketing to businesses; however, unlike a

---

typical call center, we were treated as sales professionals complete with our own private offices. I experienced tremendous success in that job, which proved to me that I have excellent telephone sales skills. Naturally that led me to believe that all phone calls would work. What I didn't know was how drastically different a cold call is versus calling a prequalified list of leads as I'd been doing. All I really had to do was get the right person on the phone and sell them.

Cold calls are another story. I started my very first outside sales job in radio advertising and spent all my time going door-to-door visiting businesses; this was in a very small town where I'd moved for a short time and locals were expected to contact locals in person, not on the phone.

That didn't work out, so I went into car sales. I did okay but didn't like it so I went back into B2B sales.

Realizing I'd never attain much as a big fish in a small pond, I bailed out of the small town and moved to a real city, where I took my first job in telecom sales. Again, I was told to cold call. They didn't care if I made those calls on the phone or if I walked office buildings. All they cared about was that I'd made my cold calls each day.

Again it didn't work. My sales manager and the corporate sales trainer assigned to our region weren't any help either; they just told me to make more calls! At this point I started to wonder if they were actually telling me to execute the definition of insanity: doing the same thing over and over with the same poor results.

This cycle was repeated a few times. I burned my way through telecom companies and colleagues started calling me a "job hopper," back in the days when that wasn't actually considered a good thing. (HR people and hiring managers now tell me that if someone hasn't moved around jobs frequently, they wonder what's wrong with that person and why they stayed so comfortable for so long, instead of getting out of their comfort zone and challenging themselves. Things certainly have changed in a very short time!)

Finally came the big interview, the job I'd been trying to get for two years. Part of the desire was emotional. As a kid on summer vacation I used to go to work with my dad at AT&T pretty frequently. His wife still works there, and I always thought I might work there someday. So it became a self-fulfilling prophecy when the best job in town happened to be with them.

Two years after first getting the attention of the local sales manager with a nicely done color trifold brochure showcasing my talents—*never* use a boring, faceless resume that looks like all the rest, or even bother with HR until *after* you accept an offer—I got a call that they'd be holding a hiring event. It was a group interview, and part of the reason the office did so well was because prospective sales reps didn't meet with the sales manager right off the bat; you had to pass this group interview first. It was designed for two reasons:

1. For the prospective salesperson to meet with both the sales manager as well as the regional manager, along with every salesperson in the office. In other words, I didn't only have to pass both managers' approval, but that of each individual salesperson as well. This was a good practice to avoid drama and office politics.
2. To put stress on the interviewee by having to speak in front of a group, as well as the pressure of doing what amounted to nearly ten job interviews all in the same evening.

After that, next came two consecutive face-to-face interviews with the sales manager. With that done, I was told they'd be in touch.

Several weeks went by and nothing was heard. I sent a nice written thank-you note to the sales manager and the regional manager for having me; however, I knew better than to beg by making endless phone calls! This would end up being a very good move, because it turns out I was about to go to work for the best sales manager I've ever had, the kind that understands that meeting with hot prospects—be they sales prospects or job prospects—is infinitely smarter and more effective than beating a dead horse.

I got the call on a Friday afternoon that I'd be leaving that Sunday for three weeks of sales training, out of state. I had to scramble to make arrangements for my dog, then packed up and got ready for my three weeks. It was three weeks of product training and zero sales training.

So what did I do? I returned home, enjoyed the weekend, then showed up for work on Monday morning, eager and ready to go. I sat down and started hammering on the phone. Then my new manager saw what I was doing and asked to see me in his office.

He went on to explain, "Frank, we didn't spend endless thousands of dollars to find, hire, and train you just to do the job of a minimum-wage telemarketer. If that's who I wanted working for me, I'd have hired one of them instead. Our people are considered true professionals. That's why as an entry-level salesperson you get the management benefit package. So start performing like one."

WOW! That was *the* single most refreshing thing I'd heard after years of being beaten up by sales managers who never actually succeeded in sales themselves, and had no clue what to instruct us to do besides cold calling.

One of the really big-time idiots had a *Wheel of Fortune*–style board he'd turn, and the various things the arrow could land on were

- Telemarketing.
- Door-to-door canvassing.
- Calling old, dead leads trying to revive them.
- Call and win back customers who left because they hate us.

And that's about it. Add more variations on cold calling or on contacting worthless leads and you'll easily fill out the rest.

Going back to the smart manager, since he could see I had been "cold calling brainwashed" he paired me up with the top sales rep in the office for a few weeks so I could learn. And what he told me was nothing of what I'd expected: "Frank, you're never going to get anywhere cold calling, trying to contact people at random on the slim hope they might be interested. The fact is that 20% of your market will never buy from you, 60% will be on the fence, and 20% will be predisposed to buy from you, but only if they know about you first. Find those 20% and let them buy."

That blew my mind. The idea that someone would actually *want* to take my call and buy was foreign to me.

The Sales Badass *only* spends valuable time on those who want to buy, or taking it a step further, those who have a need but don't realize how big the problem is.

WHY CHASING AND PURSUING ARE LOSERS' STRATEGIES

It's a well-documented fact of human nature that people want the very things they cannot have. That's the reason I unknowingly went from making 25 to 50 cold calls a day to upward of several hundred. The cold calls weren't getting me what I wanted, so what did I do? I chased even harder.

Basic mathematics tells us that anything times zero equals zero. And yet, even though the 50 cold calls each day got me nothing, I assumed that simply doing more would work better! Apparently I'd forgotten my third-grade math lessons.

Worse yet, it's typical of us humans to get what we want, then immediately want something better. Attaining the dream is never quite what it's cracked up to be, so we'll do what it takes to get our heart's desires.

The free public schools around the world are neither appreciated nor valued, because they are free! But pay $50,000 a year to have two kids in private school as I do, and suddenly there's a tremendous value placed on making sure you get your money's worth. But if you're given something free, other than a heartfelt gift from a valued friend or loved one, do you really give a shit about it?

That's why I've stopped giving books to people. People simply don't value anything they don't pay for. Inevitably everyone who hasn't done what I've done asks me where to start. And I would always give them a copy of Napoleon Hill's *Think and Grow Rich*, tell them to read it three times, then come back to discuss it, and I'll move them on to the next level in their success education.

But guess what happens—when I give it to them, *they don't read it, because it's free*! However, convincing someone to *buy* the book usually results in at least an attempt to read it, enough to have something to talk about anyway.

After my wife and I decided to have children, we also decided we needed to stop moving around (I was on state number seven and I think she was on five) and put roots down in one place.

We chose Dallas because it has a massive business community, and it's the kind of city where everyone is given a chance and anyone can succeed. It's not like some older cities where you need to be connected to get into doors, or like a fellow author I know who tried living in Boston and got nowhere because he didn't have roots there going back 200 years. Then again, maybe I should try considering my grandmother's family arrived on the *Mayflower*? (Oh wait, it's way too cold there. Never mind.)

Take a look at romantic relationships and romantic comedies and for the most part you see begging and pandering. "Honey, I know I did something wrong, but I got you these flowers. Will you please forgive me?"

Or the hopeless romantic chasing and wooing the woman of his dreams, only to keep coming back for more abuse after having been shot down a dozen times.

If there's one thing that never works in romantic relationships, it's begging the person to like you and stay with you! Hey, we've all had breakups, and we all did the same at some point when we were young and done. The reality is that attraction is not a choice. It's an automatic psychological and physiological reaction that happens in the presence of someone you're genetically compatible with. You can't make someone be attracted to you, so why do people believe this Hollywood nonsense about chasing and pursuing the person you want?

Happy couples I know didn't chase each other. They met and hit it off right away just like my wife and I did. On the other hand, in nearly all marriages where one partner pursued the other relentlessly until he or she said "yes," that partner has 100% control of the relationship and the other half gets to follow orders. The longer the pursuit carried on, the worse the marriage is for the pursuer.

This is the image that Hollywood, political correctness, and the cheap Californian psychobabble people are exposed to today. People are trained to *think* they have to chase, beg, and pursue to get what they want. Even worse is what sales managers and most sales trainers do: tell you to do *whatever it takes* to get the sale!

Friends of ours look at my wife and me and marvel at how perfect our marriage seems to be. To us, however, it's very simple: At the time we met, we had both recently decided to be "done" with dating and to take a break from the game-playing and drama for a few years.

And with no pressure, no "dates," no pretending to be people we're not, which is all a date really is after all, what started as a friendship became a near-perfect relationship and marriage with two beautiful daughters to show for it. We even like each other's in-laws. Now how often does *that* happen?

For another example, I love cars. Indeed, the primary—no, the sole—reason I even started my business, the one that led to these published books, was because I wanted a big Mercedes-Benz S500, about an $85,000 car at the time. Notice I didn't scheme or chase or beg or try to find a "great deal." I set a goal, earned the money to write a check for that goal, and went off and bought it.

Then I ordered a brand-new one a few years later. Then I ordered a new coupe a few years after that. Then I bought yet another S-Class Coupe, with a hefty price tag of $146,550, or an even $160,000 out the door with tax and miscellaneous expenses.

At that point I decided to find a new dream car, something I could aspire to in order to reach "the next level" as every self-proclaimed success "guru" calls it. Keeping in mind that I'm an interior guy first and foremost, I looked at every new Bentley. Every Rolls-Royce. I quickly learned that neither of those brands makes an interior that I actually preferred to the S550 Designo Coupe. Hey, both *Motor Trend* and *Car and Driver* declared it the finest interior ever made on any production car, ever, so don't take my word for it. I'll grant you that Rolls-Royce uses the finest interior materials found on Earth, but the boring design that's meant appeal to 90-year-olds just doesn't work for me. I'd probably fall asleep at the wheel and crash driving an elderly car like that. Oh yeah, and they're slow. (And besides, British cars just don't work right. Ask me about our Land Rover.)

Then I took a step back and considered the fact that I drive less than 5,000 miles per year, along with a lot of overhead like kids in private school, so why was I bothering with cars to begin with? I sold the six-figure Mercedes and bought a more practical five-figure Audi. It works for me and is surprisingly more fun to drive since it's nimble and not another 5,000-pound luxo-barge. And since it's cheap (by my standards anyway) I work on it and tinker with it in ways I'd never dream of with a $150,000 car. And I'm finally beating 13 miles per gallon for a change!

What's my point? The 2004 S500 wasn't enough so I had to order a brand-new 2007 S550 sedan. Then came a 2011 coupe. Then a 2016 coupe. And then that's when I realized *I would never ever be happy with any one car*, so I might as well buy cheaper ones and switch it up more often! Now many brands have programs where you pay a flat monthly payment and get to change cars as often as you'd like with other cars that are in the program. Do you see what happened there? Incidentally, the automotive industry identified people like me who enjoy switching up cars often, and came up with an entire new product offering to satisfy it. *That* is Sales Badassery. Don't just look for problems to solve—instead, create a new market to serve! And don't wait for the company to do it either. It's *your* money and *your* paycheck.

If you want to know, the desktop image on my computers is the cockpit of an airplane I want. (See, there I go on interiors again.) It's not a private jet; one of my best friends is a private jet pilot and based on his advice and seeing the kind of money pits his clients' airplanes are, I'll never own a jet when there are elite charter companies out there who can be ready to go on extremely short notice and are always on time. The airplane on my desktop is one that I want to fly and enjoy as a hobby.

I'm not spending my days in pursuit of that airplane. Likewise, I didn't chase or beg or haggle for any of those six-figure cars. I learned early in life that the person who pays full price is the person who gets full service when the time comes. The person who haggles down to a deep discount will never ever get another return phone call from their salesperson and will just be transferred to service, or the 800 number. So, I did what I needed to do in order to pay full price. And besides, when you custom order a car, they already know you want it so you're stuck with either paying full price or losing your $10,000 order deposit.

And that is why you should never ever communicate that you need *a sale!*

By custom-ordering cars, I telegraphed to the car dealer up front that I absolutely wanted the car. This destroyed any negotiating power I would've otherwise had. Naturally, I knew this would be the case and was prepared to pay full price; however, it's a perfect example of how the practice of telegraphing what you want (or need) to the other side will completely remove your leverage in the sales process. Heck, I'd even have lost my multithousand-dollar deposit if I didn't buy, so not buying would've cost more than buying in the end since I would've gotten nothing for that money!

THE WANTING-IT TAX

By making it clear up front to the car dealer each time I custom-ordered a new car, I was subjecting myself to the wanting-it tax.

The wanting-it tax is my way of explaining that once you communicate that you really want something, the price will go way up.

Imagine you're test-driving a car, and midway through you blurt out, "Oh my, I seriously love this car!"

Guess what just happened? That's right, you've trapped yourself into paying full price. No experienced automobile salesperson is going to let you off that lot without you driving off in that car.

Now if you really do love the car, but understand these principles, you'll keep your mouth shut. You'll even drop little complaints here and there and point out what you don't like about the car.

Doing that will set up the salesperson to offer a pretty good deal right up front, and then lie back and allow you to beat them down on price until they get to waste hours processing a sale just to get the $50 minimum commission.

The most egregious example of setting yourself up to get hit with the wanting-it tax is cold calling. The party in control of any interaction is the one who doesn't need anything, and the party who needs something has zero power. Guess what a cold call accomplishes? That's right, it tells the prospect that you need a sale. And then it's all downhill from there.

Likewise, those idiotic statements at the beginning of the chapter, such as, "I'll be at your beck and call if you become my customer," also make it crystal clear that you're desperately in need of a sale, and people don't like to buy from the desperate. They like to buy from the prosperous because they know the prosperous sales professional is taking great care of his customers, otherwise he wouldn't be prosperous.

You see, when you make it clear that you want a sale—worse, when you communicate that you *need it*—you just whacked yourself with the wanting-it tax. The prospect knows you need the sale, and now he's going to browbeat you down on price, and ask for all kinds of extras to be thrown in as well.

Now turn that around: You're calm, cool, and collected, giving the impression that you're secure and don't really need the sale. The prospect has picked up on this, and that bit of human nature that makes people chase what's just out of reach will get them talking about all the things they like about your product or service, just like the car buyer blew it by saying, "I love this car."

The prospect has now been charged with the wanting-it tax. You *know* he wants it, and now you're going to cheerfully take the order—at full price!

Let's take a further step back to Frank Bettger's *How I Raised Myself from Failure to Success in Selling*, published back in 1952.

In the book he talks about how he instantly doubled his sales overnight and with less effort to boot. He merely started to abandon prospects that didn't buy by the second appointment!

In other words, he got rid of the time-wasters, the people who always want to see more but never buy, and in short this idea allowed him to close more sales in fewer hours. Who doesn't want that? And what better way is there to avoid the wanting-it tax?

More importantly, his was a decision to go to a zero-tolerance policy when it comes to nonsense and a refusal to take any shit from the time-wasters. When they failed to buy by the second appointment, they got the boot—not Mr. Bettger!

In my own sales career, at the peak of my performance selling business telephone systems for the largest manufacturer in the world, the company had a 20% closing rate as a target for the sales force and this was considered an excellent number.

I closed 80%. Consistently. That's four out of five, unlike the one in five that was considered a good target to shoot for.

And the reason I was able to do that is simple: I just refused to waste time on prospects who didn't buy, first by the second appointment, and later on I replaced that second appointment with a phone call to close the deal. The phone call served two purposes: First, it saved me the time of driving to and from an appointment, waiting, presenting, and all that. Instead I emailed the proposal, which was based on my profit-justification method I'll explain later in the book, and then set up a phone call to close. Frequently I didn't even have to do that; I'd find the signed contract on the fax or in my inbox before even scheduling that call. Eventually I went to one appointment only and that's it except for very complex sales.

The other purpose, and perhaps the most important one, that this strategy served is this: By not asking for another in-person appointment and merely asking for a phone call, I came across as nondesperate. It became apparent to my prospects that while my competition was making endless follow-up calls, asking, "Have you made a decision yet?" I gave the impression that while I wanted their business, *I didn't need it.*

And that is the mindset of the Sales Badass. You of course want to close lots of business. But as far as your prospects know, *you don't need their business.*

This is so foundational to achieve Sales Badassery that I'm going to go into even further detail on both achieving and carrying out this mindset—and holding it until it becomes a part of you, because this attitude will achieve anything you want in life, beyond just sales.

I'm sure you've heard all the old urban legends about the salesman who was after one particular prospect, then finally got in after mailing him one shoe with a note that read, "Now that I've got one foot in the door, how about the other?"

Or of salespeople sending gift baskets, Starbucks gift cards, invitations to expensive steak dinners, and more wasted money just to get in front of a prospect who obviously isn't interested.

These are examples of begging, of subcommunicating, *"I'm so desperate to get a sale, that I'm going to do anything and everything to get your attention and get in the door."* In fact, I can't tell you how many Starbucks gift cards I have in my desk. I feel bad about not using them, but the idea isn't exactly original, and I don't like Starbucks anyway.

The point is that mailing me a $5 Starbucks card with a card asking for a meeting comes across as desperate to me. The salesperson just spent good money trying to get my attention! If they really wanted my attention they'd give value first rather than trying to buy my attention.

True story: When I needed a website done I put it out for bids on a freelancer site. Dozens of people around the world sent me price quotes. One web designer actually just did the site and showed me a mockup. She quoted the price and said she could have it live in about ten minutes on my server.

She got the deal! She didn't show desperation; she showed competence and a personal importance on *giving* value before trying to *get* money. It's like the old joke that as soon as you ask about vacation time in a first interview, you're out. (Yes, we really do that.)

Showing that you're desperate for a sale sends all the wrong messages to a prospect. They'll start thinking:

- Why is this person so desperate for a sale?
- Is he not getting enough repeat business, which would mean he doesn't take care of his customers?
- Is the company so broke that they can't do proper lead generation? I'm not buying from a supplier who may be out of business soon.

And on and on …

Now, when you are nonchalant, play it cool, and make it clear that you're after the business—which goes without saying since you're already working the sale—but that you don't *need* their business, opposite thoughts go through the prospect's mind:

- Huh, this is like dealing directly with the owner of the business!
- This person must be busy helping his customers if he's not chasing me down.
- This person must get a lot of repeat and referral business, which means he must take good care of customers—I'm interested!
- Hmm, I remember him speaking to my Rotary Club a while back. The man must know what he's talking about.

See? Just the opposite of what they think when you show desperation or any neediness in general.

To understand how this works, you first have to understand cat theory.

CAT THEORY

You can learn a lot from a cat.

Like how to sell, for starters.

You see, cats and dogs are very different. We have one of each in our house, and if I want the dog to come over, it's pretty simple—I call her over! Nine times out of ten, she jumps up and trots right on over, happy to see me!

The cat, on the other hand, is a different story. If you try to call a cat over, it will ignore you. The harder you try, the more you will be ignored.

She's the total opposite of the dog.

And guess what—sales prospects aren't dogs. They're cats, and if you want to get them buying from you, you need to learn and understand cat theory.

Cat theory is simple: It states that it's up to you to get the cat to come over. You're the one taking the action. However, you must trick the cat into believing that *it is the cat's own idea* to respond to you.

In other words, you're really getting the cat to come over, because you want her to. But she believes it's her own decision—that she's doing it of her own accord.

Sales prospects are exactly the same. That's why direct sales approaches trigger an instant, subconscious sales resistance in people. Cold calls are the most egregious example. Nothing is more intrusive or interrupting to a busy day.

Think about it. When you're walking through a shopping mall or other market place, and salespeople at those kiosks yell at you to come over and look at whatever useless trinket they're selling, your first reaction is to shut down and either ignore them, or say a polite "no thank you." Or maybe not so polite if they're acting like obnoxious, *desperate* losers.

By contrast, an intelligently constructed store window, containing goods you would like to have, does the polar opposite: It entices you to draw nearer, take a closer look, and possibly enter the store to buy something.

You may have thought it was your own idea to go into the store, but in reality, the store's staff made you come in. They set things up to draw you in, while letting you believe it was your own idea to do so.

That is the strategy of the winner! To lead you into buying while letting you think you actually made the decision!

That's how I got stuck paying full price for all of those brand-new luxury cars I ordered. The Mercedes-Benz dealerships don't put bare-bones cars with no options on the showroom floor because they're stupid. They do it to force people into ordering cars with the options they want. After all, it's completely pointless to have a car like that without all the high-tech gadgets—and they know there's no price haggling when you custom order a car. The effect is to make me feel powerful and important because I just handed over so much damn cash for a device to get me from point A to point B, and yet it was the dealer's plan all along.

And that's how cat theory works in the real world of selling. You must create the ideal circumstances to get prospects to come to you, ready to buy, while letting them believe they did it all on their own.

Why Does This Happen?

For dogs, it's because they love attention, and unlike cats, they're pack animals. Because they need and crave attention and companionship, they'll jump at the chance to respond to a human calling them.

Applied to sales, a dog is a prospect who desperately needs to buy your solution and doesn't even care what the price is. And how many of *those* do you ever encounter in the real world?

Cats are another story altogether. They're loners, not pack animals. They generally like to be alone. And for that reason, they neither need nor crave human attention. That's why the trick to getting a cat to come to you is to show just enough interest to let it know you're there and then pull back and ignore it. It's the pulling back and ignoring the cat that piques its interest and gets it to come over to you.

Your prospects are not dogs—your prospects are *cats*, so treat them that way!

Think of how this works in sales. If you're desperate to make a sale—say you've got too much month left at the end of the money—then you're going to treat your prospect, who is actually a cat, like a dog. And what will a cat do when treated like a dog? That's right, it'll simply ignore you.

This is precisely why the harder you push trying to get through to a prospect, or to continually call someone you've presented to, asking them if they've made a decision actually pushes them away.

On the contrary, when you conduct a professional appointment, present your solution, then lay back, your odds of getting the sale go up dramatically. There's nothing wrong with reasonable follow-up but don't call every week or something similarly needy like those "dog" salespeople do.

By doing that, you're using cat theory.

Coming out for an appointment and then presenting a solution is showing the cat that you've noticed it, are interested in it, but don't need it. This of course means that you don't try any of the time-worn closes that every decision maker has heard a thousand times, whether it's the "feel, felt, found" close or the "Ben Franklin" close or any others. You leave the solution in the prospect's hands and move on to the next.

Cat theory is the reason I have such a fantastic marriage and a truly wonderful wife who is supportive in every way, and lucky for me, she's frugal too! Our relationship is so strong because when we met, neither of us had any interest in dating, so neither of us pursued the other. We unknowingly ran cat theory on each other—and look at the result!

On the flip side, when I hear someone say they chased their wife for weeks, months, even a year before getting a date, it's a dead giveaway that the man is "whipped" and the relationship is completely one-sided. You'll hear them say it was "totally worth it" because they'll be sleeping on the couch that night if they don't. And a woman chasing a man is why so many great women who would make terrific wives end up with abusive loser jerks. People simply don't place high value on anyone who pursues them; in fact, in the science of social dynamics, pursuit is known as DLV—a display of low value.

Ignoring someone, which, granted, is a bit extreme, is a DHV—display of high value. The classic example is someone getting all giddy and overexcited meeting a celebrity, while the celebrity plays it cool. The fan is displaying low value, whereas the celebrity is displaying high value by showing low interest. It may sound paradoxical but it works, and most effectively in sales.

I personally believe the brainwashing by Hollywood romantic comedies and the glorification of a man pursuing a woman who has little interest in him is part of why the current divorce rate is so high; women want men, real men, not some pandering loser bringing her flowers and writing poetry. It probably also explains why my gym is so dead lately … one can only wonder.

Cat Theory in Sales Prospecting

Cat theory is equally important in prospecting for sales as it is in working deals; perhaps more important, because if you blow it at the onset and don't get in with a prospect, you won't even ever get to present in the first place.

The key to using cat theory in prospecting is to get prospects noticing and coming to *you*, rather than you to them.

There are several ways to do this. I'm only going to go into one in detail here because this is all covered in two of my previous books, *Never Cold Call Again: Achieve Sales Greatness Without Cold Calling* (Wiley, 2006) and *The Never Cold Call Again Online Playbook: The Definitive Guide to Internet Marketing Success* (Wiley, 2010).

Having said that, while I was pulling that 80% closing rate selling high-ticket business-phone systems, a lot of people in the office assumed I was the boss's pet or had a relative higher up in the company, or whatever their excuse of the day was that I was absolutely killing it while they rarely even made their minimum quota for the month.

A big part of that 80% close rate came from the sheer volume of highly qualified referrals, and by highly qualified, I mean they were ready to buy immediately. If they weren't, yet still wanted to meet, I politely told them I'll be happy to when they're ready to buy, which amazingly made many of them suddenly ready to buy!

Since I was selling business telephone equipment, I teamed up with reps at companies selling business telephone services, meaning PBX phone lines, ultra-high-speed Internet connectivity, and the like.

I put together a simple referral plan and made sure everyone got a copy. I made it lucrative enough that they'd be motivated. The company's standard referral program paid a bit low so I chipped in some of my commission, which made sense considering I was doing zero work to get these sales.

Every time one of those reps got a lead or an order for a new business, or a new branch office of an existing business that was opening up, they immediately put the customer and me in touch with each other and would arrange a meeting.

The suspicion from other reps in the office that I was getting free leads was caused by the fact that I'd show up at a lunch meeting with one of my referral partners along with the prospect I'd previously never met—or even heard of for that matter—and walk out with a check and a contract.

How Cat Theory Applies to That

The beautiful part about this is that those prospects never saw me as a salesperson to begin with.

By getting such a powerful introduction including a preplanned meeting, I was seen as the "go-to" person for business phone systems by them. It wasn't dissimilar from making a sales inquiry with a company and then working with the actual business owner instead of a sales rep when the time comes to buy. You simply feel more confident in the decision to buy and you have more trust in your supplier.

And, of course, someone who is referred to you by someone they trust will in turn trust you to do the right thing by them.

The same dynamic was at play when I showed up at those pre-arranged meetings. Being introduced as the consummate expert in business phone systems, along with the high recommendation of the referrer, caused the prospect to see me as a business owner of sorts and not as a sales rep.

Why?

Because no selling took place! The sale was predisposed to happen!

This, of course, is the ideal sales situation. It's also why I ask to speak to the owner of the company and not a salesperson. (No offense.) And it's something you can implement by merely figuring out who the most complementary referral partners would be for you, reaching out to those people, and putting together a nice referral-incentive plan for them.

And don't leave out your competitors in all this. No, I'm not crazy.

See, when I was selling phone systems, I worked for the most expensive provider in the market. It was very common to prequalify someone on the phone only to learn that even my cheapest solution would be out of their budget.

What did I do? Did I hang up the phone and just let that lead go? Hell no!

I knew who the low-priced players were in my market, so I went over to NEC and to Samsung and made friends with the reps there. Besides, I'd already met some at networking events.

I decided that when I got a lead for someone in need of a phone system but out of my price range, I'd send it to one of them and they'd pay me a referral fee out of their commission in return.

And they did.

Likewise, when they obtained a lead for someone who needed a very advanced solution, something that they could not provide, at least not without messing around with third-party integrations (those never go well), they'd send that lead to me and I'd pay them the referral fee based on my existing fee schedule

See how simple and easy that is?

Sales Badassery Truth

The Sales Badass is never afraid or intimidated by anyone, and certainly not by his competitors. The Sales Badass, maintaining his persona and image of power, approaches and befriends his competitors in order to make mutually beneficial deals with them.

And … be a cat yourself.

4

SALES BADASSES ALWAYS ASSUME THEY'LL WIN

> It doesn't matter how you play the game. It's whether you win or lose that counts.
>
> —*Homer Simpson*

Homer Simpson may not be much of a winner, but the Sales Badass is, and that quote is more true in sales than in any other profession.

In sales there are no "participation" trophies. You either win or you lose. If the best you can do is to try your hardest and show good sportsmanship when you lose, you'll wind up broke, unemployed, and bankrupt.

That's why there's no second or third place in sales. You either do or die.

And that's why Sales Badasses *never* see losing as an option. *Not ever.*

For a real-life example of this, consider Donald Trump in the 2016 presidential campaign. Whether you love him or hate him—and it's always one or the other—is irrelevant. The point is that his supreme confidence and his undying belief that he would win, even when the odds were stacked so far against him that he was considered as having no chance at all, brought him to victory.

Then he was sworn in as the forty-fifth president of the United States.

Why?

Because he always *believed* he would win! That's all there is to the Trump story of election success!

We've all been taught about goals, but how much do we really practice goal setting? Moreover, how much do any of us really practice the principle of autosuggestion—repeated self-suggestion of a thought, idea, or goal—until it becomes reality?

Here's a bit of hard truth: If you are *not* writing down your sales goals, making them lofty, and most importantly, reading them aloud at least twice daily while feeling and envisioning yourself achieving those goals, *you will not achieve them.*

THE POWER OF AUTOSUGGESTION IN SALES BADASSERY

Autosuggestion, as I just mentioned, is repeated self-suggestion to the point where the idea suggested becomes a true belief, and then becomes a part of the individual's persona and at that point the subconscious mind takes over, working on ways and means for the goal to become a reality.

To demonstrate, let me tell you a story (this is from memory so details won't be exact, but it still gets the point across):

Many decades ago, a young man who had saved several thousand dollars over a period of years, and who had brilliant visions on how his employer's business might grow immensely, found himself in an unusual opportunity. The company was in bad shape and was to be sold to creditors if someone with enough capital couldn't come along to save it.

The young man looked at the sale price then looked at his bank account, and saw a difference of $10,000.

He set out to raise the $10,000 from investors. He worked his group of customers who were loyal to him because he *provided them with value and service* above and beyond what they'd paid for.

By the time he worked his customer list and those of family and friends, he came up $1,000 short, with only 24 hours remaining to either come up with the rest of the money or lose it all (the money raised thus far had to be deposited toward the sale in order to avoid losing the business).

Knowing he'd come this far after so much blood, sweat, and tears spent, and knowing the loss of both his money and the business was imminent, the young man sat down and closed his eyes and repeated to himself for hours, "I'm going to find that $1,000 before the deadline tomorrow."

With that, he drove himself home when he saw a light on in one lone office on his town's main street. With a flash of inspiration— *from the idea he had just burned into his mind through autosuggestion*—the young man marched into that office, explained the entire story from start to finish, and walked out with the final $1,000 he needed!

That is the power of the Sales Badassery goal-setting mindset.

PRACTICAL GOAL SETTING AND ACHIEVEMENT

First of all, forget the sales manager garbage of "Figure out what number you need to make, then divide that by the average dollar amount per sale, then multiply that by the number of proposals it takes to get a sale, then multiply that by the number of cold calls you need to get enough proposals submitted, and you have your number! Divide by the number of working days in the month and that's your daily cold call number."

NONSENSE.

The Sales Badass knows that's garbage, because if it were true, employers would pay per cold call rather than for closed sales! Seriously, any time you hear that crap, ask the employer to put their money where their mouth is and pay you per cold call made. Watch how fast they backtrack.

What the Sales Badass does is decide on what sales number he wants as a goal for the month, which should ideally be 200% of quota or more since goals nearly all fall short, and then *burns that number into his mind along with undying belief that he will achieve it.*

There's no reverse engineering the final number to determine the number of cold calls and appointments and proposals needed. *There is only the number and the belief that one will attain it.*

There are any number of ways to take your goal number and use autosuggestion to first believe that you will achieve it, and then to *know* that you will achieve it.

I prefer the Napoleon Hill method: Write down your goal, the timeframe for its acquisition, what you intend to give in return for it (in this case, your services as a sales professional), and read the statement aloud twice daily, once in the morning and once at bedtime, seeing and feeling yourself in achievement of that goal.

Others say to write your goals down twice a day, others say to keep them written on a pocket or wallet card and look at it throughout the day, but regardless, just do it! Decide which method works best for you and then become a true goal-setting (and goal-achieving) Sales Badass.

"IMPOSSIBLE" SALES EASILY CLOSED WITH THIS MINDSET

Similarly, a new sales rep in an office was greeted by the others in the office, and the veteran sales "pros" decided to play a trick on him.

They offered him a nice list of leads to get him started, and the new rep happily accepted them. What he didn't know was the trick that was in play—those leads weren't fresh leads, they were leads that even the very best sales pros in the office could not close, and in some cases, couldn't even get into the door.

Before going out to visit those prospects, he stopped in a park, sat on a bench, and closed his eyes and repeated to himself 100 times, "I'm going to sell every one of these prospects I visit today."

And he did!

When he returned to the office, the pros all had smirks on their faces waiting to see how dejected he was from being shot down by all those difficult prospects. They were in absolute shock when they learned just how many of those people he'd closed!

When the pros asked how he did it, he simply said, "I believed that I would sell them, and I did."

That is all there is to the Sales Badassery mindset of sales closing success!

OVERCOMING YOUR LIMITING BELIEFS— SALES BADASSES HAVE NONE

You guessed it—more psychology! I feel like instruction on overcoming limiting beliefs was widespread when I began my sales career, but since I haven't seen it mentioned anywhere in recent years I'm going to cover it here.

The reason for spending time on some of the psychological background of Sales Badassery is because I firmly believe that in order for the techniques to really work for you, or your "outer game," as I call it, you must first get your "inner game" in order, and most importantly, you must get rid of the limiting beliefs you have in your mind that are probably holding you back from achieving great success.

Your subconscious mind is always at work. Day and night, while you're awake and especially while you sleep, your subconscious is always thinking and processing information. The problem has to do with the fact that it cannot differentiate between positive and negative—it merely works with the information handed over to it from the conscious mind—and because it never stops working, if it has nothing other than negative thoughts to work with, it will.

Information and thoughts can only be handed over from the conscious mind to the subconscious if they are continuously repeated in the conscious mind and emotionally charged. The idea of self-suggestion or autosuggestion is the process of repeating a thought to oneself, over and over again in a state of emotion, until it finally reaches the subconscious and is acted upon.

The effectiveness of this process has been known for over a century and has been proven in various studies. For example, in one study, smokers who had repeatedly tried to quit and failed were given statements and were instructed to say these statements several times out loud in front of a mirror immediately upon arising, once during the course of the day, and, most importantly, immediately before going to bed at night. They were to say these statements as emotionally as possible and to really feel the power and emotion behind the message as strongly as possible. The statements went something like this:

Smoking is a filthy, disgusting habit. Only the most worthless, low-down people smoke. I don't do it because I hate it, it disgusts me, and inhaling the lethal fumes makes me physically sick. It's even killing me. I can't stand the smell and the taste is downright repulsive. Just the thought of a cigarette makes me nauseous to the point that I want to vomit. I hate smoking.

The subjects who followed the instructions to the letter and repeated the statement to themselves with strong emotion were unable to even pick up a cigarette after a few weeks of this. These are people who had been trying to quit, unsuccessfully, for years, keeping in mind that nicotine is considered to be more addictive than even heroin.

Most people inadvertently cause this same principle to work against themselves, and they usually manage to do it while they're trying to help or improve themselves in one way or another. This is because of a lack of common knowledge about the internal workings of the human mind. It was the belief of Andrew Carnegie, Thomas Edison, and many other successful people that these principles should be taught in school and, if they were, they would cut the average time needed to complete school in half.

Here's an example of how salespeople cause this principle to backfire and actually cause more harm than good. The problem lies in the fact that salespeople give themselves directives that cause the subconscious to dwell upon and therefore amplify the negative. Let's consider some things an up-and-coming salesperson might ask him- or herself in an attempt to improve:

"How can I overcome my fear of rejection?"

Although salespeople who ask this question of themselves don't realize it, it causes the mind to focus on *fear* and *rejection* rather than on positive virtues. Keep in mind that any thoughts that reach the subconscious mind are accepted by it, processed, and the end result is fed back to the conscious mind for the purpose of being put into action.

Asking oneself how to get over fear and rejection causes the subconscious to recognize the key points of *fear* and *rejection,* which then feed back to the conscious mind ways and means of feeling even more *fear* and *rejection,* thereby paralyzing the salesperson's mind with these emotions and destroying any chances for success.

"How can I overcome frustration in day-to-day selling?"

Once again, this is a question that focuses on a negative virtue, in this case *frustration*. After a salesperson spends enough time thinking about it and asking the question of him- or herself, the idea of *frustration* will eventually reach the subconscious mind through the principle of autosuggestion. The subconscious will act on it and send back to the conscious mind an even stronger feeling and fear of *frustration*.

"How can I avoid feeling stupid or doing dumb things in sales situations?"

Here, the salesperson is inadvertently using the principle of autosuggestion to feed the ideas of feeling stupid and doing dumb things to the subconscious. Guess what? The subconscious acts upon it and gives the conscious mind instructions about how to do even more dumb things and how to feel even stupider, and that's exactly what happens.

Your subconscious mind is like a fertile garden spot that always manages to fill up with weeds if you don't keep it filled with desirable crops. Anyone who keeps a garden or takes pride in having a beautiful yard knows there are always a few fertile spots where no matter what you do, weeds just seem to keep popping up. That's because fertile soil is fertile to any kind of seeds that happen to land there, no matter what they are. It cannot differentiate between good and bad seeds. That's exactly how your subconscious operates. It takes whatever is fed to it and works with it, good or bad. It's your responsibility to make sure that only good, positive thoughts reach your subconscious mind and to keep the bad, negative thoughts out.

How to do this? One of the simplest and most effective ways is to be on guard for negative thoughts, questions, and self-doubts, and to reframe them in a positive light. Reframing is the process of taking a negative perspective and asking the same question from a positive point of view. Let's use the aforementioned examples to demonstrate this:

"How can I overcome my fear of rejection?" might become "I'm happy to hear 'no' because it means I'm closer to 'yes'" or, even better, "Who cares what happens? In every situation I'm indifferent to the outcome." This reinforces, in your own mind, the fact that you don't need anyone's business. You want it, but certainly don't need it. This will change your subcommunication—the body language and vocal intonation that literally make it true that how we say something is more important than what we even say. Prospects will pick up on the fact that you don't need their business, and that part of human nature that wants what is not obtainable will cause the prospect to want to give you the sale.

"How can I overcome frustration in day-to-day selling?" might become "How can I be happy and in a good mood during my day-to-day selling?" or, even better, "I feel healthy, I feel happy, I feel terrific, and nothing bothers me, ever."

"How can I avoid feeling stupid or doing dumb things in sales situations?" becomes "I'm the best at what I do and am an expert. I inspire awe and respect from the people I do business with." Or, you might even say to yourself, "I don't care what anyone thinks of me regardless of what the outcome is, because it doesn't matter anyway."

Write a positive statement about yourself. It can be as simple as the "I feel healthy, I feel happy, I feel terrific!" famously used by W. Clement Stone. Repeat your positive self-image statement to yourself throughout the day, but most importantly right before you go to sleep at night, preferably as you lie in bed.

It is especially important to feed positive thoughts and images to your subconscious mind right before you go to sleep because your subconscious works hardest while you sleep. The thoughts you think before falling asleep will determine, to a large degree, how you feel when you wake up in the morning and how your entire day will be. When you have a bad day, it's almost certainly because you thought about problems or worries before going to sleep the night before. Think positive at bedtime at all costs!

This principle of carefully directing your thoughts before going to bed at night is also the reason many motivational speakers and coaches recommend reviewing your to-do list and your next day's activities right before going to bed. It allows that information to be processed by your subconscious mind as you sleep, and in many cases you'll wake up with fresh, new ideas that will contribute to your tasks that day. When you have seemingly brilliant ideas that seem to flash into your mind from out of "thin air," that's your subconscious mind talking to you.

Interestingly, Thomas A. Edison had the solution for the incandescent electric lamp handed over to him by his subconscious mind in a dream as he napped one day. Mr. Edison slept only three to four hours every night and took several 15-minute naps during the day to make up the deficit. The problem at the time was that he could get a wire to glow as an electric current passed through it, but the wire would burn out very quickly. During one long, particularly frustrating day in which Mr. Edison failed at several attempts to build a light bulb and prevent the wire from burning out, he drifted off to sleep. As Mr. Edison fell asleep, he had a vivid dream of a piece of wood burning brightly and quickly reducing down to ashes. His dream then shifted to a piece of charcoal underneath the ashes continuing to glow for a long time. As he awoke, he realized that the wood quickly burned down to ashes because it was exposed to oxygen but the charcoal burned brightly for hours because it was choked off from the air. He immediately took a piece of wire, put it inside a jar, pumped out all the air, hooked it up to an electric current, and at that very moment the world's first incandescent electric lamp was born, a product of the creative vision of Mr. Edison's subconscious mind, which was hard at work on the problem as he slept.

MENTAL MOVIES

In developing my own habit of always believing that I'd close every sale I went after, I used the technique of mental movies, where you see the victory happening in your mind over and over before the real thing, combined with assuming a powerful persona in my mind.

What I used to do fairly consistently to keep my confident persona up was to watch the movie *Wall Street* on a periodic basis and imagine that I was Gordon Gekko. This had many effects.

First, it got me dressing like Gordon Gekko. And it wasn't expensive either; you can emulate any look you want if you know where to shop. This revealed to me the psychology of good clothes that I covered in Chapter 2, and I began to see its effects immediately. Interestingly, all along I assumed it was the clothes that were making the impression on prospects and inducing them to buy, but once I read Hill's book I realized that the clothes were making the impression on *me*, not them!

Second, it got me to acting like Gordon Gekko. Not obnoxious, not back-slapping and calling everyone I met "pal," but just a very overwhelmingly confident state of mind. And that state of mind became part of my own persona, part of who I am.

Finally, it got me into the mindset of winning. Often you hear phrases like "get the business" or "earn the business" but no one in sales talks about winning versus losing, presumably because losing is too politically incorrect in today's society of "participation trophies" and rewarding those who don't try and subsequently don't win. (Seriously, what happened to the competitive spirit?)

Now I've realized I've gone off on a tangent; I do that, in case you haven't noticed already, though it's always to make an important point. Here's the most important thing that my Gordon Gekko persona did for me:

When I would mentally rehearse sales appointments, I not only played the movie in my head with everything going right and me getting the sale at the end, but I also *saw myself as Gordon Gekko* in those mental movies.

And guess what happened? That's right, I *became* Gordon Gekko in sales appointments!

Is it any wonder, then, that I managed an 80% close rate when everyone else was praised if they hit 20%?

THE PSYCHOLOGY OF GOOD CLOTHES, REVISITED

The primary point of using the psychology of good clothes is the impression it makes on you, not necessarily the impression it makes on others.

Keeping in mind that I usually work from a private office where I cannot be disturbed, on days when I have something very important to do, or an important call that could mean a lot of money for me, I still dress to the nines *even when no one else is going to see me!*

Why? Because of the impression good clothes make on *me*. They transform me into that persona of having unlimited confidence and absolute, steadfast belief that I will win.

Professional telemarketers—the kind who close five-figure, high-ticket items and services on the phone, not those people who annoy you at dinnertime—know and understand this principle. That's why they also dress to the nines in order to perform their best, and even keep a mirror in front of themselves to be sure they're smiling during the entire conversation, because smiles can be heard in a person's voice even without seeing them. And you now know the importance of a genuine smile in gaining likeability!

LIMITING BELIEFS COMMON TO SALESPEOPLE

In the research for my first book, *Never Cold Call Again: Achieve Sales Greatness Without Cold Calling* (Wiley, 2006), I spent time visiting with and talking with experts on the science of social dynamics.

What I learned was the polar opposite of what I was taught by sales managers, which was this: Each rejection brings you closer to a "yes," and, more important, each rejection and each "no" helps to build thick skin and make you immune to rejection once you've conditioned yourself against it.

When I met with those behavioral experts, however, I was told the opposite: That repeated rejection *creates a downward spiral and actually makes you more afraid of rejection and more timid around prospects.*

Looking back over my sales career, I agree with the second statement. In fact it explains the sales phenomenon knows as "getting on a roll" or "getting in a rut."

When we get in a rut, it's because repeated rejection and failure feeds on itself. Each time we hear "no," we get beaten down a bit more. And with each successive failure, our confidence diminishes a bit more. Eventually we get to the point where this constant rejection comes through in our subcommunication, body language, and vocal tone. Prospects can pick up on it, and for all the same reasons they don't want to work with a desperate salesperson, they don't want to work with an underconfident one either.

On the other hand, when we get on a roll, it's because repeated victory also feeds on itself! It's an old sales adage that when you win a sale, you should immediately get on with seeing the next hot prospect in your sales funnel. That's because you'll still be glowing from your prior victory, and that prospect will feed on your confidence and enthusiasm and *want to buy* from you!

"But Frank, what if I don't have any recent victories to feed on? What then?"

Simple! Practice mental movies. Pick a powerful persona, whether it's Gordon Gekko, or your favorite president, or a character who works best for you.

Become that character in your mind, and play out the mental movies of you arriving at the sales appointment, showing up powerful, being treated with utmost respect not only by the prospect but also by the rest of the office staff, and finally closing the deal with zero resistance and walking out with a signed contract and check.

That is exactly how you "get on a roll" when you're not on one already! Think about it. How does the switch from rut to roll happen in the first place? Usually, when we're stuck in a rut and then finally make a sale, it's because we got a call-in lead, or someone else with an urgent need to buy right now.

The victory and feeling of confidence from making that sale overtakes us, and it carries over to the next prospect. And next. And next. Then you're on a roll.

And how do rolls usually end? For me, it was always because I'd sell so much over a period of a few months that I'd eventually spend an entire month working with customers on fixing problems, whether they were installation problem, billing errors, or what have you. (Keep in mind this was in corporate America where almost no one seems to do their job to the fullest, hence all the problems.)

Listening to all those yelling, angry customers, then spending time with my own company's belligerent, lazy staff, led to negativity, which settled into my mind as a negative mental attitude.

Being beaten up by those customers and my own company's lazy support people was just as bad as losing sale after sale after sale.

And hence a rut began.

The way out was always the same: Use the psychology of good clothes combined with taking on an imaginary yet powerful persona, and use mental movies to retrain my mind to think positively, always got me back to closing sales and getting back on a roll again.

Remember, the Sales Badass doesn't think he'll win. He doesn't even believe he'll win. When it comes down to it, he knows he will win. So use these ideas to find the way that's best suited to you to make your goals come to life, and come to know that you'll achieve them, because then you will!

Sales Badassery Truth

Sales Badasses achieve virtually unimaginably high sales numbers because they set goals, plan, and internalize those goals until they cannot be stopped.

5

SALES BADASSES
ARE POWERFUL TO
THE VERY END

Selling and Negotiation Are One and the Same

A PRIMER ON NEGOTIATING

> If you think you have power, you have it. If you don't think you
> have power, even if you have it, you don't have it.
>
> —*Herb Cohen, negotiating expert*

Negotiation is all about power. Like Herb Cohen said, power is strictly about thought. To partially rephrase his quote, even if you *don't* have it, but *think* you do, *you have it.*

And hence whoever has the power in a negotiation will win. Every time. The key, however, is showing up as powerful—having it before the negotiation even begins—and then the hard part, keeping it through to the very end.

A great example of keeping power from history is of Ronald Reagan's famous, or infamous, walkout on his summit with Soviet Premier Mikhail Gorbachev.

Reagan showed up powerfully; in fact he didn't wear an overcoat, but just a suit, in the subzero temperatures, leaving the Soviet people watching on television thinking, "Who *is* this man?"

But it's how he kept his power that's remarkable. It turns out that Gorbachev failed to keep some promises he'd made at the previous summit.

What did Reagan do in response? He famously stood up, jabbed Gorbachev in the chest with a finger while saying, "You lied," then walked out altogether.

Summit ended. Game over.

The Soviet Union fell shortly thereafter. They simply didn't bring as much power to the table as Reagan did, couldn't match his power at the negotiating table, and therefore they lost.

The same is true with sales. Whoever brings the most power to the table—and manages to keep that power—will become the winner. But first we must define winning and losing in sales:

Winning, to the prospect: Either getting rid of the salesperson by getting him to accept no for an answer or buying the product at a very steep discount that guts the salesperson's commission. (By the way, conceding to a deep discount almost guarantees a problem customer down the road; those who pay full price are rarely heard from.)

Winning, to the salesperson: Closing a sale at a high price and earning a nice big fat commission.

There's really no conflict of interest here. This isn't a zero-sum game, as Gordon Gekko described the US economy in *Wall Street*. Every sale has the potential outcome of being a positive, win-win outcome for both the buyer and the salesperson.

For that to happen, however, two conditions must be met:

1. The prospect must have an actual, current need for what you're selling. This is why I'm so adamantly opposed to cold calling; it's because cold calling tends to get appointments with time-wasters and the kind of prospect who is always "exploring options for next year," or telling you to "check back in another six months," whereas highly qualified prospects tend to respond to marketing instead.
2. The salesperson must be supremely powerful, which is the focus of this chapter.

WHAT IS POWER IN SALES?

Power in sales is not being intimidated by prospects. To take things a step further, it's seeing yourself as equal or superior to your prospects. And maybe even intimidating them.

Most importantly, it's thinking like a business owner or executive.

Obviously, a big part of that is how you dress. Think of a CEO when you see one speak on television. Could you imagine that CEO addressing the press in a golf shirt and khakis? Or are those CEOs always in tailored suits, presenting an image of power?

Likewise, do you picture a powerful CEO wearing a beard or with a trendy, hip haircut? *No!* The working principle here is professionalism. There's nothing wrong with having either, however, only if it's appropriate to your job or profession. If you're selling 18-wheelers to trucking companies, that's one thing, but if you're selling $250,000 phone systems to VPs and CEOs, you may want to reconsider for the sake of your job and financial security.

(TIP: If you're a man and want to feel like the ultimate badass, take after me and learn to use cut-throat straight razors. Once you get good with them you'll really feel like the ultimate badass! Plus it's an enjoyable zenlike morning routine for me.)

Or think of the people who your prospects typically turn to for advice. Attorneys are one of the first who come to mind. Now granted, most lawyers I know wear jeans when they don't have court or are not seeing clients, but would they dare meet with a client (or prospective client) or show up in court in jeans? Never!

Lawyers work hard to maintain an image of intimidation. That's because people want tough, no-nonsense lawyers representing them and the clothes fulfill this image, and it's why "legalese" still persists—since the majority of state legislators along with members of Congress are lawyers by profession, they write the laws to favor, well, lawyers.

The dark suits with red power ties and slicked-back hair and the "legalese" that mere mortals cannot understand are means by which the legal profession maintains its image of power and intimidation. With that in mind, what's *your* excuse for not maintaining that kind of image?

The same is true with doctors. Although the nurses and office staff wear scrubs, the doctor wears the signature white lab coat. This conveys power—it frames the doctor as the authority figure in the room. This is why far too many people simply follow doctors' orders rather than asking questions and being healthily skeptical. (No pun intended!)

So why aren't you practicing similar power strategies?

Did I intimidate prospects as a salesperson? Yes, I frequently did. When I lived in Phoenix and would wear a suit when it was 115 degrees out, which made me the only salesperson in the city wearing a suit in that kind of heat, virtually no one else I met with wore a suit. (Except lawyers, though I was frequently assumed to be one. Seriously.)

Given all the new construction that was going on at the time, and the fact that I sold business telephone systems, I frequently found myself on construction sites meeting with a supervisor in a hardhat and getting the specs for the phone system proposal.

Initially I was afraid that this might alienate them but that didn't happen. It made me stand out and it made them call me when the time came to buy.

Most importantly, *I dressed like the people they turn to for advice.* In the case of someone working on a new development project, for them that usually meant a banker. So, I looked like a banker. A high-powered one. And it worked. It may have worked even better than with other prospects, because developers don't go to bankers necessarily for advice—they go to them for money! (Now that's *real* power.)

POWER IN NEGOTIATION

In negotiating, determining who will win in advance is easy. It's the person with the power.

And how is that power defined?

The person with power is the one who doesn't necessarily need anything. The person who is not in power is the person who needs something, or in this case, needs to win more than the other side does. And that need subcommunicates itself as a lack of power.

More specifically, a need is communicated by making the initial contact and requesting a meeting. Power is communicated and displayed by being the person responding to such a request.

This is why I've written multiple books about how to generate leads and sales through self-marketing instead of through cold calling. When you make a cold call you communicate your need to make a sale to the prospect, and that immediately gives the prospect all the power in the situation and sets you up to lose.

When you employ self-marketing, on the other hand, you get qualified prospects to proverbially raise their hands and make that first initial contact, letting you know they need to buy something you happen to offer.

See how simple yet profoundly powerful and outcome-changing that is?

I'm not going to cover lead generation here—I already have in previous books—but it's a prime example of how and why salespeople set themselves up to fail even before they begin trying.

Imagine a Sales Badass—or any person with a lot of power and confidence. Can you picture that person cold calling? Can you honestly imagine him or her "dialing for dollars" and "smiling and dialing," calling strangers at random, with the slim hope that one will accept an appointment?

Of course not. I sure as hell can't. Because Sales Badasses don't submit themselves to such humiliation, nor are they stupid enough to give away their power before the sales process even begins.

KEYS TO POWER AND SALES SUCCESS

1. **Dress powerfully**. Remember, forget the garbage advice to "dress like your prospects." Dress *like the people they turn to for advice* instead.

2. **Walk and talk powerfully**. This will be explained in detail in an upcoming chapter, but just remember George W. Bush's quote when asked about the funny way he walks: "In Texas, we call it swagger." Walk with swagger no matter your stage in your sales career or your level of success!

3. **Create and implement a self-marketing plan** to generate leads for you without the need for cold calling; this gets people raising their hands to show interest, even if this is as simple as someone entering an email address on a website. Author and marketing expert Seth Godin wrote that we're now in a "Permission Economy" that has made cold prospecting obsolete and where getting people to "raise their hands" for

you to express interest is absolutely essential for twenty-first-century sales success.

4. **Show up with a powerful mindset and assumption that you'll win.** You can accomplish this mindset using the techniques outlined in Chapter 4.

5. **Don't tolerate interruptions during a presentation.** Although it's perfectly natural and also necessary to allow for questions during a sales presentation or a proposal presentation, when the prospect interrupts with a question, jot it down and calmly say, "I'll address that when I finish." And then make sure you do.

6. **Don't take *any* shit from prospects.** If you're in an appointment and the prospect keeps interrupting you by answering the phone or anything else, close your notepad or binder, stand up, and confidently say, "Let's reschedule this meeting for when you can give me your full attention." I speak from personal experience when I say that prospects immediately turn off the phone and do give their undivided attention for the rest of the meeting. (Translation: You just made the prospect your little bitch and you will win.)

   Likewise, if you show up on time for an appointment—preferably five minutes early—and you find yourself waiting and waiting, don't tolerate that. Instead, inform the receptionist that you have other people to see that day and you'll reschedule when your prospect can show up on time. (This again makes them your little bitch.)

7. **Don't allow prospects to insult you.** I've had my share in the past (particularly when I was in my early 20s and hadn't learned these principles of power yet), who would make disrespectful comments such as, "I guess you really need this sale judging by that car of yours," or something to that effect. Finally, I learned to stand up, announce that I don't have time for that kind of

disrespectful bullshit, tell the prospect to grow up, and walk out. You'd be surprised at how often they'd follow me out to make amends or call back the same day or the next day apologizing and asking for another appointment. Of course, at that point I'd seized all power from them, leaving them powerless and walking out with a nice sale.

And, since I can't say it enough, look, walk, and talk the part!

Sales Badassery Truth

The Sales Badass wins by never chasing or begging, showing up with power, and remaining more powerful than the prospect in order to get the sale at the desired price.

6

WHY SELLING IS A LOSER'S STRATEGY

People hate to be sold but they love to buy.

—*Jeffrey Gitomer*

It's true. I hate to be the bearer of bad news, but the truth is clear: Selling is for losers.

Why? Very simply, it's because you're, well, *selling*.

I define buying and selling differently than most people.

To me, buying is a pleasurable process where you happily exchange money for something you want or need.

Selling, on the other hand, is an uphill process of trying to convince someone that they want or need what you have. It's all about overcoming objections, coercion, manipulation; I'm getting a headache just thinking about it!

Selling is a tough job and a losing battle. That's why salespeople suck at it. Likewise, being sold is not enjoyable to a customer. That's why people have built-in sales resistance, that's automatically and unconsciously triggered at any attempt at selling them.

A while back, author Neil Strauss came out with a book called *The Game* (Harper Collins, 2005) about his experiences in spending a few years with an underground society of so-called "pickup artists" who essentially boiled dating down to a science. Having met Neil a long time ago at a marketing event, I couldn't resist checking out the book, and it was interesting.

He tells the story of how women, who are approached by extremely attractive men they desire greatly, routinely reject them anyway— just because of how they approach the women!

In other words, they got rejected because they're basically selling instead of using a better approach.

And guess what—you're doing the same with your sales prospects. You may have a great product, at a great price, that performs a great service for your customers.

But if you're *selling* you're not going to get anywhere.

The very best salespeople—the six-figure earners—*never* sell. Instead, they create the circumstances for buying to take place, and sit back and *simply let people buy.*

HOW TO SUCCEED IN SALES

Of all the varieties of selling, from rookie mistakes all the way to sleazy dishonest tactics and so-called "closes," the worst of all is cold calling.

If you look at my definition of "selling," cold calling definitely takes the cake. It makes it practically impossible to let people buy.

If you want to succeed in sales, and become a top-performing salesperson almost immediately, there are two steps you must take to make that happen:

1. Stop selling, and start creating circumstances where people buy.
2. The first step to that is to stop cold calling because it's the worst form of selling.

Take those steps, and watch your sales numbers explode and your stress disappear!

WHY AVOIDING SELLING BENEFITS SALES BADASSES

As you know by now, every sales interaction is a negotiation, and in negotiating, the person who holds the power—or "holds the cards," to use the vernacular—will win every time. Every time.

That's why it's so critical to change your mindset from someone who is supposed to sell and convince people to buy something that they may not need or even want, and instead to induce people to simply *buy* on their own will.

Regardless of how you look at it, anytime you're in a tense sales situation, overcoming objections, bragging about your features and benefits over the competition, and then trying to rely on sleazy "closes" to get the sale, it's because you're trying to *sell*. You are not with someone who is being induced to *buy*.

Going back to cat theory for a moment, consider what's happening in a typical sales appointment as I just described: You're treating the prospect like a dog. You think that holding out enough treats and the lure of amazing features and benefits from your product or service is going to convince your prospect to buy.

However, the problem here is that you're treating the prospect, a cat, like a dog. And cats don't respond to the same stimuli that dogs do.

You'll never in a million years get a cat's undivided attention and affection by trying to call it over like a dog.

(And besides, it's just rude to treat your prospects like dogs. Sheesh.)

When you're selling, you're doing all the things that repel the cat. Instead, what you need to do is slow down, relax, and subcommunicate that you don't need the sale. You don't have to even say it; when you do exactly that, the prospect will also feel more relaxed and will go into a "buying" state of mind rather than expecting sales pressure, getting it, and then shutting you down completely.

If you have trouble doing this, spend some time in the car deep-breathing. I won't go into breathing exercises here since there is an endless amount of info online about it; however, I can promise you that it really does calm you down both mentally and physically.

Now what I'm about to say may come across as sleazy, but hey, I'm a Sales Badass and it worked every time, and on top of that it created tons of very happy new customers for me.

In my phone system days, I worked for the premier company in the industry and naturally that came with the highest price tags as well.

When a prospect would start spitting out price objections that I knew weren't true (which you'll learn how to detect in an upcoming chapter), I'd come back with a calm, cool, collected, "That's okay, I understand that we're the most expensive provider in the industry and that not everyone can afford our products."

Well … that got prospects on the defensive! It frequently resulted in a best-case scenario in which full price was paid in order for the prospect to prove that the business could indeed afford it. And in a worst-case scenario, I still got the sale, not at full price always but certainly for a lot more than the deep discounts the prospects demanded.

That may sound a bit pushy and even insulting, but hey, it worked, at least in B2B sales. I didn't dare say that when I sold cars for the simple fact that if the person really can't afford the car, all I'd be doing by making that statement is insulting and hurting the person. However, if I were selling a brand like Rolls-Royce, then of course I'd use that statement to close deals; after all, who has any business taking up the valuable time of a Rolls-Royce salesman if he can't even buy the Rolls? Not to mention the fact that early on in my car sales adventures, I learned that the big money is in economy cars and pickup trucks. Luxury cars frequently had the lowest margins and commissions because affluent buyers tend to be more savvy and better negotiators. But in the end I avoided getting the $50 minimum commission on those cars by turning things around on the prospect and challenging the fact of why he or she is shopping high-end cars if they can't afford one.

See what I did right there? That's a prime example of a Sales Badass refusing to tolerate any nonsense or time-wasting from prospects. Selling cars involves very long days and hard work, not to mention abuse from prospects who assume the worst coming in. If I'm selling a high-end car and someone is wasting my time knowing they can't pay for it, then I'm sure as hell going to try and qualify them out very quickly so I can avoid wasting my time on an unqualified buyer and move on to one who is qualified.

Believe me, if you haven't sold cars, you'd be shocked at the amount of people who come in and fill out a credit app, trying to qualify based on their welfare checks. I refused to have my time wasted by them. Hence the friendly, "So, what do you do for a living?" early in the sales interaction.

THE SALES BADASS IS VERY HANDS-ON

One of the first things I learned selling cars was that to get a sale, you needed to get the prospect in the car test-driving it.

So that's what I did. I'd ask questions to get an idea of what someone was looking for, then suggest we take a specific car for a drive. Even if they didn't like the car, getting them driving got them eager to try out more cars and it was only a matter of time until they drove one that they couldn't turn down.

Likewise, in the business phone system industry, we always tried to get a demo in somewhere along the line, where the prospects, including the decision maker along with the receptionist and several employees who use the phones, to try them out for real.

Even though we did have a mobile demo kit, it was huge and heavy to lug around, so I always requested that my prospects come to my office.

This served three specific purposes. First, and most obvious, we could do a better job of doing a demo in the actual demo room that was already set up in the office. Everything was preprogrammed and operating just like a normal business phone system complete with dial tone.

Second, and more importantly, it got the prospect following my directions. Getting a prospect to follow my lead and come to my office, rather than theirs, shifted the power dynamic in my direction and gave me the power in the sales process, and, as you well know by now, whomever has the power wins.

Third, and perhaps most powerfully, the company receptionist and others who use the phones heavily are invited to the demonstration. When they tell the boss they like the new phones over the old ones and want them, the boss is pretty much stuck making the purchase in order to keep important employees happy and loyal. And if you think a receptionist isn't an important employee, think again. The receptionist is the face and the voice of the entire company. This is so critical that I actually know of a dentist whose practice went under because his obnoxious and rude receptionist was driving patients away! Sadly, he had no idea because he wasn't paying attention, and he paid the price for it.

THE YES LADDER

Have you ever heard of a "yes ladder"?

That's the old sales theory that states that the more you can get a person saying yes to random and even irrelevant questions, the more they'll get into the habit of saying yes and ultimately buy.

While this strategy is hardly foolproof, it's certainly a valuable addition to your arsenal of Sales Badassery tactics.

Earlier I mentioned Neil Strauss and his book *The Game* (HarperCollins, 2005). In his story of spending years in the so-called "Secret Society" of pickup artists in Los Angeles—yes, this is a real thing—one of the techniques they'd use on women out in bars and clubs was the yes ladder.

It was a simple matter of making conversation, primarily consisting of stories, true or not, that you script and memorize ahead of time. The stories are supposed to be extremely interesting, real-life anecdotes of things you've actually done or experienced, in order to hold attention.

Part of the process of opening a conversation and jumping into your routines was to work on the yes ladder—get them saying yes!

Now for a short tangent: One thing I've said probably thousands of times in books, articles, and email newsletters is that human nature is human nature and all sales are the same. All people respond to the same buying triggers as everyone else.

That's why I got so frustrated when I'd apply for a sales job in another industry. I was sometimes shot down for lack of industry and/or product knowledge, despite the obvious fact that selling is selling.

In fact, the other superstar salesperson beside myself in our region knew absolutely nothing about the product he was selling, and yet he performed at exceptional levels.

The issue was the training we were sent to for three weeks prior to going out in the field. There was literally zero sales training. It was product training. We had to complete tasks like programming a series of features handed to us on a piece of paper into an actual telephone system.

I mean, seriously, since when are salespeople suddenly technicians who program phones? That's what the techs are for!

Back to the story. I wasn't there to see this, but I'm told on good authority by other reps who were at that training that the star salesperson was out partying late each and every night, and would show up for class each day hungover and wearing sunglasses and would sleep through most of each day.

In other words, he learned nothing about the product. Yet he sold tons of it, to everyone's amazement. That's because *he was already successful in sales.* He knew what made people buy, and he did it. He's living proof that industry and product knowledge is entirely irrelevant if you know and understand what makes people *buy.*

That's because all sales are the same. Human nature never changes. And if you continually remind yourself of that fact, while implementing the techniques presented in this book, you'll lose a lot of your limiting beliefs about sales and about your own capabilities and will see an astonishing rise in your sales production.

GOING UNDER THE RADAR FOR EASY SALES

Let's revisit Neil Strauss's book, which was about a group of men calling themselves pickup artists, whose sole purpose was to perfect the art of picking up women in bars. I keep coming back to it because these guys studied and employed the science of social dynamics, the very same set of social dynamics that work well in sales. It's also a good reminder that sales skills are valuable throughout all of life and not just in your business or professional life.

Here's the gist of what they did: They'd approach women in bars and open conversations with dumb questions about random things, always starting with, "Hey, I need a female opinion on something."

What this did was allow them to come in under the radar. As the book explains, in a bar or nightclub situation, women automatically have their guard up and the usual pickup lines that men use will fail, even if the woman would otherwise be interested in the man. They call this a programming wall.

Sound familiar? Thinking back to what most prospects are like initially, can you just feel the programming walls that went up between the two of you?

But by using this strategy of asking a completely random question, under the guise of "I need your opinion," they'd be able to start a conversation and move it forward to where they could successfully get a phone number or get her out on a date.

What intrigued me most, however, was this idea of programming walls and how a woman would not talk to a desirable man, just because he approached her in a way that hit one of these subconscious walls and caused her to shut down.

It intrigued me because selling works in exactly the same way. Selling is a game of human nature, and you have to know how to make the right approach and avoid hitting these so-called programming walls.

SELLING AND PROGRAMMING WALLS

I observe myself doing it all the time. Whether I'm walking through the mall and pass by one of those kiosks with an annoying salesperson calling me to come over, or a sales rep approaches me in the typical cold-call manner, I completely shut down and want nothing to do with them.

Sometimes I even do this with the friendly people offering free samples in the supermarket—not because I don't want the sample, but because their method of approach triggers a programming wall in my mind, and I walk on by pretending I didn't hear. Their calling out to me instantly triggers subconscious memories of pushy salespeople— and the end result is that I want nothing to do with them even though I don't know why. After all, they're giving away free stuff!

Similarly, someone may be selling something I need or something I am even actively shopping for, but when they cold call me, the programming wall goes up, they slam head first into it, and nothing happens. The same is true in a sales appointment when I'm clearly ready to buy (I won't accept a sales appointment unless I am) and then the rep jumps into the company story and all sorts of nonsense that no one wants to hear.

In fact, I remember hiring a call center company at one point to handle my inbound customer service early on. I did my Internet research and decided on this company before I'd even picked up the phone. My decision was made; I was ready to buy.

Then the rep who was assigned to me did all the wrong things. Specifically, she practically demanded that I hear out the company story. She even tried to barrel over me with it on the phone and then sent it to me again via email.

I didn't read it and didn't care. I ended up just contacting the business owner so I could get started on their services without all that sales bullshit.

So many times, I've had to listen to the company's latest iteration of their sales process. These varied from stupid shit such as a mandatory three-appointment sales process for a service that only took one appointment or even just a phone call to close, all the way to "gates and hats" where you had to recognize which "hat" the prospect was wearing at any given moment and what "gate" they were putting up between you and them.

I mean, really, really stupid shit. The worst was when a company brought me in to figure out why they weren't making their numbers. I immediately learned that they had a mandatory 21-step sales process that every rep was supposed to follow.

21 steps! No matter that no one ever bought! Prospects probably couldn't kick the reps out fast enough!

Years ago, a sales manager who agreed that cold calling is a waste of time explained to us that cold calling is slamming head first into a brick wall, when we really needed to go *around* the walls.

That's why even those who cold call will still perpetuate ridiculous stories about how someone "got in the door," like the urban legend about mailing someone one shoe along with a note saying, "I've got one foot in the door, how about the other?"

Obviously, someone who has never sold successfully made that one up, but you get my point—getting in the door successfully means finding ways and means of getting around the door and into the decision-maker's office.

Now forget cold calling for a moment and think about sales in the big picture.

Selling means slamming into that door over and over again. If you follow the insane advice to increase your activity, that only means is that you'll be slamming into it even more and more. Remember, selling represents an uphill battle of trying to convince someone to buy, rather than the pleasant and stress-free process of them simply buying from you on their own accord.

Seriously, it's not that hard. Not for a Sales Badass, anyway. Make the prospect instantly like and trust you, don't tolerate any nonsense, be a boss, and keep the power through the sales process, and you'll win most every time.

The answer isn't to sell, it's to create the proper circumstances to get people to want to buy. Then just sit back and let them buy. It's really that simple. And when you combine all the information in this book and begin to employ it, you'll find that prospects really do love to buy, and can't wait for the chance to do so.

Sales Badassery Truth

The Sales Badass never goes for a hard sell but, rather, creates the ideal circumstances to make people want to buy.

7

Boldness Is for Losers: Sales Badassery Self-Confidence

Walk tall and carry a big stick.
—*Theodore Roosevelt*

There's a blog I tried to like. It's geared toward men and is about general business success as well as physical fitness. In other words, the exact things that interest me.

However, I have one big problem with it; it includes the word *bold* in the title.

This completely discredits the entire blog for me, because as a Sales Badass I know the difference between boldness—that is, fake confidence—and *real* self-confidence.

Here's an example: Two people are going skydiving. Of the two, one jumper is bold while the other is confident.

The bold jumper yells, "Hell yeah, man, this is going to be awesome, I so totally can't wait do to this! WOOHOO!"

The *confident* jumper gets up, gets ready to go, and simply says, "Let's do this."

See the difference?

SHOW ME, DON'T TELL ME

Being bold in the example is clearly nothing other than a big macho show. By putting on a highly animated show, yelling about how pumped up he is and is so excited, what that bold jumper is really doing is subcommunicating fear. After all, why else would he need to psych himself up if he weren't afraid to jump? Answer: He wouldn't.

That's the problem with boldness. It's "all bark and no bite." Or as Texans say, "all hat and no cattle."

The confident jumper didn't do that. By remaining calm and collected—cool if you will—that individual demonstrated real confidence without having to say a word about it.

Remember my example of the calmness and coolness of celebrities when meeting a fan, whereas the fan is doing the exact opposite and showing an unusual amount of excitement? That's a display of high value on the part of the celebrity, and a display of low value by the fan.

And that sums up boldness. It's nothing more than a display of low value. If you want to display high value and make yourself irresistible to prospects, forget the boldness and be cool and confident.

Picture the stereotypical salesperson shown on television shows. It's almost always a loud, boisterous, back-slapping type of person. That, to me, is not professional, nor is it confident. It's a display of boldness, and you now know that boldness is the polar opposite of confidence.

It reminds me of some people I've encountered in the world of entrepreneurs and business.

For example, I've had to listen to one who couldn't talk about anything other than, "Look at my Rolls-Royce! I have a private jet! Check out the pictures! Look at my new beach house!"

Needless to say, I couldn't get away from him quickly enough, and felt like I needed a shower after.

Similarly, I know someone else who got the vanity license plate "Bow Down" for his Lamborghini. In reality he's an extremely kind, friendly, and generous man, someone I consider a friend, but a Lambo screams "douchebag" as it is, let alone without "Bow Down" on the license plate! (No offense intended against Lamborghini owners!)

What these people don't understand is that by acting the way that they do, people instantly and automatically apply the label "asshole" in their minds.

People make assumptions about the things they see. A lot of assumptions. For example, I live in Dallas proper, not a suburb, and as a result I'm only a couple of miles from where those like Mark Cuban, Ross Perot, George W. Bush, and many other wealthy people live. In fact I even see them out and about quite a bit, right down to having had conversations with Ross Perot in the barbershop. (When I asked him about Trump, he was neutral politically and simply said he respects his business accomplishments. Fair enough.)

I make it a habit of driving through those neighborhoods on a regular basis, at least twice a week, for inspiration. Seeing those monster mansions and huge properties makes me irresistibly want one, and desire is the seed of all achievement!

And when I say monster properties, I mean there are more than a few that dwarf Mark Cuban's house, just to put things in perspective. And that dude is a *billionaire.*

When I would drive through there in the $150,000 Mercedes-Benz, I felt like I belonged and people would recognize that and assume I was one of them.

Indeed, it didn't work out that way.

What actually happened what that people would ignore me when I smiled and waved (in Texas we all smile and wave at each other), or worse yet, even snarl at me!

Then I downgraded to the Audi I'm driving now. (Which wasn't all that much of a downgrade,to be honest.) I felt self-conscious not being in a Bentley-expensive vehicle and thought I would be typecast as another wannabe gawking at all the big $40 million properties.

However, that's not what happened. Indeed, now they smile and wave back at me, and even do it to me before I do it to them! And the only difference is I'm driving a sub-$100K car versus a $150K car. Then again, the number-one selling vehicle to US millionaires is the Ford F-150, so maybe they're onto something after all.

It goes to show that even the very wealthy and successful, with tons of life experience, make false assumptions about things they see. It's clear that people assumed I must be an asshole driving that pricey car. (And now that I have the Audi, when I see the occasional picture of the top-end Benz, it really does look obnoxious to me now that it's been gone a while.)

Worse yet, I made the wrong assumptions about *those people*. When they didn't wave back I assumed *they* must be assholes. As it turns out, that wasn't the case at all, and in fact very wealthy people I know happen to be the kindest and most generous people I know.

Let me tell you another story:

Growing up, I was always an introvert. I know this is hard for my current group of friends to believe since I've become so outgoing, and my wife, who I met over 14 years ago at the time of this writing, still doesn't believe that I was ever an introvert!

But the plain truth is that I was, and I hated it. I didn't have the self-confidence to interact with new people. As a kid, when relatives would come over to visit, I'd go hide in my bedroom upstairs. Seriously!

Then, moving forward into my sales career, in my early 20s, I was still like that to a significant degree after I'd started in sales, and even after I became a star producer.

I was visiting family one time and my grandfather kept shaking his head, wondering how on earth I could be great at sales when I was so quiet.

He said to me, "To be good as a salesman you need to be able to talk and be pushy and be a showman and bullshit people and all that."

Well, as you know, that's not what a true sales professional does, and certainly not a Sales Badass. We sure as hell don't bullshit people. Sales Badasses are straight arrows.

There's an old saying that you have two ears and one mouth for a reason: So you can listen twice as much as you talk. Personally I think you should listen even more than that. I know I do.

And that's what made my introverted old self do so well in sales. I listened far more than I talked. In fact I didn't even realize I was techniquing prospects by keeping my mouth shut, since it caused an uncomfortable silence and the prospect would go right on talking again to fill the gap.

Keeping the prospect talking while keeping my mouth shut did something very important, something essential to Sales Badassery: The prospect inadvertently told me every reason why he wanted and needed the product!

Now if I had kept my mouth running, or stood up to give a boring presentation, or went through the "steps of a sale," there's no way in hell I'd have achieved the same level of success.

That's why the television stereotype of a salesperson is dead wrong, and worse yet, it fools salespeople who watch into believing they should be behaving the same way! Then when they do it, it comes across as very off-putting to prospects and kills deals dead in their tracks. The reason is twofold: First, the salesperson didn't get the prospect talking endlessly, and therefore never found out what the prospect wanted or why. Second, it is simply obnoxious. Talking and barreling over someone who has a need that you're obligated to fill isn't just rude, it's unprofessional, and it's a failure to do your job properly.

But that's fine. When you see what acting like that does to your sales numbers and your employment status—or business status if you're self-employed—you'll stop that in a hurry!

Sales Badassery Truth

Sales Badasses are confident at all times and leave the "boldness" to losers.

8

Sales Badasses *Never* Seek Approval

Stop Chasing and Start Getting

Let me explain to you why salespeople almost inevitably wind up seeking approval and even end up chasing after it.

One thing I routinely see when training salespeople is an inferiority complex. I've mentioned the television and Hollywood stereotypes of salespeople that contribute to this. With or without that, however, it's usually there, because salespeople are led to believe that the prospect is the boss and the salesperson is there to serve.

Although this may be partially true—you certainly do need to serve your customers *after* they buy—it gets salespeople seeking and chasing the approval of prospects when in reality they could just as easily show up as an equal or a superior and never have to deal with any of that nonsense.

You sure as hell are not obligated to serve anyone who hasn't paid you and become your customer, so don't give in to their demands that you do.

In my case, what happened was that I went into sales, got my first outside sales job, went off to sales training, and was ordered to cold call relentlessly.

Now you know my opinion of cold calling. It doesn't work anymore in our twenty-first-century, Information Age economy. There are simply too many ways for prospects to find what they need on their own, which is why they no longer accept cold calls and why you need to position yourself where prospects will see you and proverbially raise their hands to show interest.

Having said that, I didn't know any better at 22 years old and just made the cold calls. Whether it was on the phone, going door-to-door, or what have you, I made at least a hundred a day. I remember walking buildings and hitting every office and sometimes doing that until 7:00 in the evening, feeling exhilarated, and believing the old sales trainer myth that I'd "planted lots of seeds" and would soon get to reap the benefits.

For some reason, it didn't seem to work out that way.

What actually happened is that I was hung up on and had doors slammed in my face day after day after day, complete with being yelled at and thrown out of offices. I've even had the police called on me once. This wore on me and it had a lasting, negative effect on my self-confidence. I was told that after hearing no enough times, it would just naturally start to roll off me like water off a duck, but the exact opposite happened. Over time I became terrified to make those cold calls. I finally became paralyzed with fear and simply didn't do anything at all, which led to a lot of job-hopping because I wasn't making my numbers. (By the way, that's where the bizarre morning ritual of "lead sorting" comes from—the paralysis of inaction.)

Remember that discussion about sales rolls and ruts? This kind of nonsense is exactly how one gets into a sales rut. I mean, what worse thing could there be for a salesperson other than total inaction? But that's what happened to me when I was continually beaten down with rejection, all because I took the stupid advice to cold call people all day.

I started saying desperate, idiotic things like, "What will it take to earn your business?" (Remember that one?) I began seeing prospects as superiors, because, after all, they were in charge each and every time. They must be; after all, why else would they have had the power to shoot me down all the time?

Here's what happened as a result:

The continuous rejection damaged my own self-confidence to the point that it quickly became apparent, through my nonverbal subcommunication, that I'd been beaten down into a spineless, supplicating, typical annoying salesperson. Like all the others who would come calling, I became just another faceless salesperson with nothing of value to offer. At least to them, anyway.

> Even the devil hates the man with a rubber backbone, for he smells bad burning!
>
> **—Napoleon Hill**

Experts have said that as much as 93% of person-to-person communication is nonverbal. Now that figure varies wildly, from that high of 93% down to numbers as low as the upper 50s in terms of percentages.

Either way you look at it, nonverbal cues still make up the majority of our interpersonal communications.

And when you've been hammered on relentlessly, day after day, believe me when I tell you it *will* show in your nonverbal communication.

What is nonverbal communication? It consists of body language, vocal intonation and volume, our facial expressions, not to mention much more subtle communication we unknowingly transmit and that the prospect unknowingly interprets through his or her subconscious mind.

Have you ever had the feeling that, upon meeting someone for the first time, you simply didn't like that person? Odds are you had no idea why—you just had a gut feeling about it. Your brain was saying, "Get away," and you did.

After being beaten down with endless rejection, I began giving off those same subtle, nonverbal cues, and the effect was the same. Prospects wanted nothing to do with me.

I was coming across as a *loser* and people only want to work with *winners*. That's just a hard fact of life that you must accept and adapt to. Like death and taxes.

Be a winner.

"The Reality Factor" states that fighting reality is difficult, painful, and ultimately fruitless, while accepting and adapting to reality is easy and will make you successful. So let's just be done with denying reality and see the real world for what it is—a rough-and-tumble place to be in the business of selling. In other words, you must come across as a winner in order to succeed. That's just the way it is, so let's just adapt to that and work with it to your advantage, because being a loser is, well, a losing strategy.

"JUST A FEW DOLLARS"

I once read a story explaining why money, or lack of it, can profoundly change a person's outward appearance to others, by dramatically influencing that person's subcommunication.

It talked about an unemployed man who was looking for a job. He still had the same nice car, still wore the same high-end, finely tailored suits, and otherwise looked just like everyone else, but there was something in his walk, in his eyes, in the tone of his voice that communicated failure to all those he came into contact with.

He'd walk down city streets, looking into businesses and envying the people who had secure employment. He felt empty without a definite purpose to aspire to every day.

George W. Bush, when he ran for president, famously said, "In Texas we call it swagger" when someone commented that he walks funny.

Well, the man in the story certainly didn't have swagger. He had shuffling feet, a slight slump in his posture, a look of defeat in his eyes, his head hung low, and all the other cues any potential employer would pick up on, decide there was something about him they didn't like, and turn him down for a job.

The only difference here is money. If the man had a few more dollars in his pocket, things would change, but without money, and the associated success and security that comes with it, his demeanor changed from one of a successful man to that of a failure.

Likewise, having sales coming in gives you a tremendous amount of self-confidence. You'll naturally walk with swagger without even realizing it. Your head will be held up high. You'll have a smile on your face, or a serious look of definite purposefulness. You'll move briskly because you have places to go and things to do. And *that* is what gets you on a sales roll. It's why one of the very best pieces of sales advice ever given is to get out and see prospects the moment you close a sale—your success and enthusiasm will be contagious and you'll get more sales as a result!

Now, are you beginning to see the similarity between the man in the story, and how a lack of sales will drag you down?

Without sales coming in, you'll transform into the man who needed just a few more dollars if you're not careful. That's why it's so important to practice the body language, likeability formula, and other details in this book if you want to become a star salesperson.

Worst of all, you'll become too available. This may sound paradoxical in the world of sales, where you need to be ready to go pick up a deal when the prospect is ready to buy; however, being *too* available is a display of low value.

Once I'd become a veteran salesperson and hung out with the other star producers in the office, it became a running joke to watch the rookies get a lead, or manage to get an appointment via a cold call, and haul ass out to their cars and rush to the prospect's location.

Inevitably they'd come back with that signature look of defeat in their eyes and no swagger in their walk, because the prospect wasn't truly qualified. They were just looking.

That's why those of us who did extremely well would challenge an interested prospect! That's right—we didn't jump in the car and rush over, we challenged them.

How?

By attempting to qualify them *out.* Although it's a natural reaction to want to visit an interested prospect as quickly as possible, it's also the wrong reaction. What it communicates to prospects is that you have too much free time on your hands, not enough deals in the works, not enough happy customers giving you referrals...and in the end that gut feeling that there's just something about you they don't like will kick in.

On the other end of the scale, when I had an interested prospect on the phone, I'd immediately ask what their budget is. Naturally, most refused to say because they assumed I was trying to figure out how much to price my proposal for maximum profit. (I wasn't.) What I was doing was, first, making sure I wasn't wasting my time on someone who couldn't afford to buy, and second, I was subcommunicating that *my time is valuable and the prospect will need to earn my time.*

(By the way, in case you're wondering, when they'd refuse to tell me their budget, I'd get some basic info and throw out a ballpark figure on the higher end of the scale. That quickly got rid of the unqualified prospects.)

By making a declaration that your time is valuable, in this case an indirect declaration, what happens is that good old-fashioned human nature kicks in: The more you make them work to get to meet with you, the more desperate they'll become to *want* to meet with you—and buy!

Never forget that human beings want what we cannot have. When something is given to us free, we don't appreciate it. We only appreciate and desire the things we have to work for, to earn. Likewise, prospects *don't* desire to meet with a sales rep who will drop everything he's doing to jump in the car and speed over. They *do* want to meet with someone who is obviously busy and has a lot on his plate, because that's the hallmark of a successful salesperson.

There's an old saying that if you want something done quickly and correctly, give it to a very busy person, because they get stuff done.

Continuing on with this theme, I didn't rush to call people back. I had a policy, which I still teach to salespeople: If someone leaves you a voicemail in the morning, call them that afternoon. If they leave a message that afternoon, call back first thing the next morning.

Why?

Because you appear to be a busy person with a lot going on, and as we all know, busy people are successful people! Think about what impression a busy salesperson makes:

- He is out closing tons of deals.
- He has a large book of customers to take care of.
- He gets tons of referrals from those satisfied customers.
- He is financially comfortable and not desperate for new business.

And much more. Overall it is a powerful display of high value.

The salesperson who has endless free time to respond instantly to prospects displays the opposite—a display of low value by being too idle and not busy enough. And no one wants to do business with someone who displays low value. After all, if you have low value, how on earth can you bring value to someone? You can't!

APPROVAL-SEEKING BEHAVIORS

There's a long list of approval-seeking behaviors as you might imagine, so I'm going to cover the most important ones first:

- Asks what it will take to earn the business, and similar begging-type statements.
- Ends sentences with "right?" or "you know?"
- Drops everything to go see any mildly interested prospect, even lukewarm ones.
- Allows prospects to run the sales appointment instead of the other way around.
- Uses excessive hand gestures when talking (there's a lot of debate on this one, but per the science of social dynamics, lots of hand gestures or otherwise moving around while talking is a release, and therefore a display, of nervousness).
- Makes relentless follow-up calls, pestering the prospect about whether or not they've made a decision yet, instead of moving on to highly qualified prospects who are ready to buy now.

You get the idea. I could go on and on, but for the sake of brevity, let's work on these specific areas of approval-seeking behavior.

Much as limiting beliefs are reversed by writing them out in a statement, then writing a new, positive statement to replace them, Sales Badasses replace loser behavior with winner behavior.

For example:

- Instead of asking what it will take to earn the prospect's business, or promise to be at their beck and call, the Sales Badass works to qualify prospects *out*, and, instead of making those idiotic, approval-seeking statements, seeks to learn the buyer's timeline and who else will be involved. (Sales Badasses only meet with decision-makers. Only!)
- The Sales Badass never ends a sentence or statement with, "Right?" or "You know?" Instead, each statement is confidently ended with the appropriate vocal intonation down.
- The Sales Badass seeks to qualify prospects *out,* rather than meet with anyone who is willing, and strategically times return calls and emails to avoid looking desperate.
- The Sales Badass is in charge and runs the show. If a prospect is taking phone calls or otherwise being inconsiderate and/or not paying attention, the Sales Badass terminates the appointment and tells the prospect to let him know when he'll be free without distractions. Likewise, if the Sales Badass is made to wait very long past the scheduled appointment time, he'll leave and re-schedule.
- The Sales Badass speaks confidently and is like a rock—no endless hand gestures.
- The Sales Badass doesn't do the stereotypical activity of calling to ask if a decision has been made only to be blown off over and over again. He knows that if the prospect was going to buy, it would, and he moves on to more high-value prospects.

In other words, what the Sales Badass is doing is displaying high value. Meanwhile, losers display low value, and that's why Sales Badasses kick their ass at sales.

DITCH YOUR SECRET EXCUSE

Everyone has a secret excuse or did at one point; I've managed to get rid of mine.

For me it was the fact that I'd dropped out of college after only one year. When I got into sales, I found myself working with nothing but college graduates, and indeed the jobs I held technically required one. (Thankfully my sales record spoke for itself.)

Likewise, I got out to networking mixers, got involved politically, and did what I could to make contacts. Inevitably, the next question asked after, "What do you do for a living?" was always, "Where did you go to school?"

I'd always sheepishly answer, "I didn't." Of course that impresses people now that I'm a *New York Times* best-seller, but back then I had no social or economic status and I let it damage my self-confidence. I'd back out of group conversations after that came up and go find someone else to mingle with, only to have it happen again.

Why did it matter?

The beautiful truth is that it didn't! However, you wouldn't have been able to convince me of that at the time. For me it was just more rejection and being looked down upon, on top of already getting beaten up every day in sales.

My lack of so-called education became my secret excuse. Like the alcoholic who uses his alcoholism as an excuse to hang onto the bottle and keep on drinking, I used my lack of a college degree as an excuse for my failure and wondered what the hell my life would turn into, because at the time, it seemed pretty damn hopeless. The only jobs I could get were in sales, and I wasn't even making it there. This was all because of society's reaction to my lack of a college education.

The dating game wasn't helping me, either. My introversion was a problem as well as the lack of self-confidence I was experiencing as a result of continued rejection, in both my business and my personal lives. Okay, so I'm good-looking. I'll give you that! However, I'm of below-average height, and when people are in their early twenties, they're at their shallowest in terms of whom they're willing to date. (By the way, don't worry—I'm nowhere near as short as Vladimir Putin. That dude has a major Napoleon complex.)

So I made a decision, no doubt inspired by one of the hundreds of self-help books over the years: I decided to get over my height and prove to myself that it didn't matter. That meant pursuing taller women. And to my shock and amazement, when I approached them with confidence, they didn't reject me! This became so ingrained in me that taller women became my preference, and now my wife is taller than me. It's amazing how strongly the mind will manifest thoughts that are fed to it, isn't it?

Now think about how powerful that is in terms of feeding your mind positive thoughts, thoughts of achievement and success, rather than thoughts of defeat and anxiety and failure.

My experience with taller women was a huge eye-opener to me. I'd always been led to believe that attractive women only like taller men.

But guess what—that myth is a *classic secret excuse used by men who fail with women because they won't put in the work to improve themselves*!

Powerful stuff, these secret excuses!

I call it the brainwashing. Human beings are gullible creatures. We're naturally trusting and want to believe that what we are told is true. (Really, who likes being lied to?)

As a single twenty-something I was brainwashed to believe that I'd have to settle for whatever dates I could scrounge up because I was too short.

As a young, naïve rookie salesperson, I was brainwashed to believe that if I'd just put in enough effort—just make enough cold calls—that I'd reap the rewards of my hard work, yet it never seemed to work out that way.

So I turned it around and began the "reverse brainwashing." I took all those limiting beliefs and turned them on their heads. I dated two different six-foot tall blondes and three different fitness models. Then I obliterated the sales world by overturning those limiting beliefs and, as if by magic, I became a star in the field of sales, including the top rep in my company's entire region.

Just like endless rejection feeds itself into an endless downward spiral, *endless victory feeds itself into an endless winning streak!*

As I wrap up the writing of this chapter, I'm coming to realize that it may be the most important chapter in the entire book. Study it. Reread it. Learn it. And then use it.

Sales Badassery Truth

Approval-seeking behavior is the ultimate display of low value. Never seeking approval but rather expecting and accepting it—and giving people reasons to give it to you—is the ultimate display of high value.

9

SALES BADASSES ARE HUMAN LIE DETECTORS

Know Which Objections Are Real and Which Ones Are Bullshit

WARNING: *Do not* attempt to use these techniques in your personal life, especially with your significant other. Everyone has secrets, and if you detect deception when they deny them, your relationship will be in big trouble. *Only* use these techniques in the world of business and sales.

Objections seem to be the bane of most sales professionals. Entire books have been written on overcoming objections, but how can you possibly overcome an objection if you don't know if it's true or if the prospect is lying or throwing out token objections to get rid of you?

For example, the biggest problem objection is price. "We can't afford it." "It's not in our budget." However, most of the time, price objections are bogus. The prospect is either trying to worm his way out of buying from you, or they're trying to get a deep discount that isn't helpful to either you or your company.

Since salespeople struggle with price objections and few are adept at overcoming them, how valuable will it be to know if the price objection is real or not?

That's where deception detection comes in. The strategies in this chapter were learned from CIA interrogation techniques; those officers are very adept at detecting lies when someone is talking, and what you're going to learn here is a big picture version of what they do, limited to the techniques that matter most in sales. There are entire books written on this topic.

The polygraph, popularly known as the "lie detector," doesn't detect lies at all. What it does is measure breathing, pulse, and sensors to detect sweat on the skin. The actual "lie detection" is done by the polygraph operator, who must interpret what he sees on the graphs and then determine what answers were true and which ones are lies.

Similarly, the techniques I'm about to show you work as well as the polygraph however, just like the polygraph, you will need to interpret and process what comes out of a prospect's mouth and determine whether that objection is true or if it's just a stalling tactic—in other words, a lie.

Here's the glue that holds this all together: *When listening and trying to determine if the prospect is lying, you need to ignore and not process truthful statements.*

Remember the fact that communication between human beings is both verbal and nonverbal? That means deception can come in either form, so you must listen well, just like any competent sales professional, but you must also look and observe the prospect's body language.

Furthermore, you cannot rely on just one or the other. We consider that deception may be happening when more than one red flag goes up. And those combined behaviors may be both verbal and nonverbal, so it's essential to listen well and watch the prospect like a hawk.

Once you see two or more deceptive indicators, you can assume that there's a high probability that the prospect is lying, and that leaves you with some more work to do—let the prospect talk while you observe. Ask questions to keep the prospect talking. The more cues you can pick up on, the more accurately you'll know if the prospect is telling the truth or not.

DETECTING LIES: QUANTITY OVER QUALITY

The key to knowing if someone is lying or not is to watch for multiple deceptive indicators. If there's only one, ignore it, since that's not enough to rely on to make an educated guess.

However, if there are two or more, you have more work and questioning to do. But if there's a large amount all at once—what CIA interrogators call a "cluster"—then you can be confident that the prospect is lying to you and use that knowledge to destroy the objection and close the deal.

THE VERBAL DECEPTIVE INDICATORS TO WATCH FOR

Now let's get into the specific deceptive behaviors and indicators that you need to learn, memorize, internalize, and then use to defeat bullshit objections and close more sales.

1. **Failure to Answer.** If you ask the prospect a question and you don't get a direct answer, that is a strong deception indicator. (Remember, though, that it takes more than one since just one could be a fluke. Maybe the prospect didn't understand the question, or heard you wrong.)

Failure to answer includes answers to your questions that are completely irrelevant and don't answer your question. Another is a long pause or delay before answering. That means the prospect had to take time to think of something to tell you in order to put up a wall between the two of you. If the answer were truthful, the prospect would have given the answer immediately.

2. **Lack of Denial.** This is somewhat similar to failure to answer the question. For example, if you ask the prospect if they really can't afford your solution and you don't get an immediate no, you're dealing with lack of denial. The prospect said your solution is too expensive, yet didn't immediately deny that fact when you repeated it back to him in the form of a question. If you get anything other than an explicit denial, that may be a deceptive indicator. Here's an example:

Prospect: "This is way too expensive. You need to do something on price before we can make a deal."

Salesperson: "So what you're saying is that the company can't afford it?"

Prospect: "Well, we have to look at our budget and I need to talk with my associates to see if it is or not."

Did you notice what happened there? If the prospect were being truthful, he would have immediately answered, "No, this really is beyond our budget for this." But he didn't do that. Instead, he gave you an answer with a lack of any direct denial, and you got a stall tactic from the prospect. Of course the decision-maker knows the budget and whether they can afford the purchase. If you don't get a direct answer, they're potentially lying—remember, you need more than one deceptive indicator—or they really don't know, which means you're not in front of the correct person. Remember, Sales Badasses only meet with the person who can sign the contract, never with a go-between like an office manager or executive assistant who has no possible way of delivering the presentation and closing the sale nearly as well as you can. Not even close!

Diving deeper into denial or lack of denial, there are two more indicators to watch for. The first is the nonspecific denial. For example, if the prospect gives a vague or very broad answer rather than just saying no, you're looking at a nonspecific denial. They denied that they can't afford it, but instead of simply saying that, you hear something like, "Well, we have to get two more bids before we can make a decision."

That is a nonspecific denial. Instead of giving you a direct no, they gave you what essentially is an excuse not to buy right then and there.

The other is the long-winded no. If the person does give you a no but it's part of a long-winded answer rather than a direct and brief no, that's significant. It's a big red flag for deception.

3. **Refusal or Failure to Answer.** I know you've probably heard this one a million times: "I'm not sure I'm the right person you should be talking to." With this one, there's a 50/50 chance that it's either the truth or a lie. The way you determine whether it is a lie is to watch for other deceptive indicators. If you get more than one—including this one—then you can assume the prospect is most likely not telling the truth.

The reason this is a 50/50 indicator is that you don't know right off the bat if you really are talking to the wrong person or if you are talking to the actual decision-maker but he's trying to blow you off. That's why it's incredibly important to look for multiple red flags and not just rely on one. Some people simply have habits of speech and/or body language. For example, most body language books will tell you that if someone is crossing their arms while talking, they're not interested in talking to you or they're lying.

However, some people just like to do that! I know I do when my arms need a rest, so again, don't jump to conclusions because of just one clue.

4. **Repeating the Question.** Silence in response to a question is almost certainly a deceptive behavior, and a strong one; if you get this one along with one or more others, you can be fairly certain you're being jacked around and they're trying to trick you into giving up. However, someone who isn't telling the truth will hate the awkward silence, and instead will repeat the question back to you in order to give himself some time to think of a bullshit answer to your question.

Behavioral psychologists have determined that people think about ten times faster than they talk. That means by repeating the question back to you, although they're only buying maybe ten seconds or so, in terms of thought process that's well over a minute and a half in "brain time." And that's a lot of time to come up with an excuse to not buy.

Always remember, maybe the prospect really didn't hear you or understand the question fully. That's why it's important never to assume deception unless you have *multiple* indicators coming at you.

5. **The Nonanswer Statement.** A person will give a nonanswer statement for the same reason they would repeat a question: to buy time to think of excuses and bogus objections to throw at you.

Politicians do this all the time, and you'll notice this all the time if you follow politics at all. They make nonanswer statements, such as:

"I'm glad you asked me that question."
"You know, that's a very interesting question."
"I'm happy to answer that for you."

"That's certainly a legitimate concern."

(That last one is *very* common in sales.)

In reality, none of those statements are actually true. They're stalling tactics to allow the person to think and come up with the answer in his head while verbally stalling you.

6. **Inconsistent or Contradictory Statements.** When someone gives you an answer, or simply makes a statement on their own, then says something later that's either inconsistent or contradicts their earlier statement, that's a strong deceptive indicator.

It's been said that telling the truth all the time is best because you don't have to remember lies and add to the stories to make them believable.

So when someone says two or more things that are not consistent with each other, you can be fairly sure that the person is making up lies as he goes along and isn't doing a very good job of tying everything together to make it believable. Trying to keep your story straight as you go along is a difficult thing to pull off, hence this is a strong deceptive indicator. (Remember though, you need more than one!)

7. **Attacking You.** This is when the prospect is essentially backed into a corner and can't come up with anything believable, so they attack you. I know I've been told things like:

"How long have you been doing your job?"

"Didn't you even research our organization before coming out?"

When you hear attack questions like this, know that the prospect has nothing else in his arsenal and is resorting to attacking you rather than just answering your questions.

In interpersonal relations, this is usually heard as something similar to, "Why don't you trust me?" Again, please do not use any of this on your significant other. Far too many people have and figured out things that they probably didn't want to know, and had the relationship fail as a result. This is powerful information, so only use it appropriately.

8. **Irrelevant Questions.** It's not necessarily true that answering a question with a question is a deceptive indicator, but if the question you get in return isn't directly related to your question, that's a big red flag.

   For example, if you ask a prospect a question that's specific to their needs and your solution, and they come back with, "What is the penalty if we cancel the contract?" you've got a strong deceptive indicator on your hands, not to mention someone who doesn't intend to remain your customer!

9. **Answers That Are Too Specific.** This one happens when someone answers a question with far too many unnecessary or irrelevant details.

   People do this in order to try to make themselves look good. They're trying to gain your favor by giving you more than you asked for. However, as I said, they're only *trying* to gain your favor. In reality, truthful answers are direct and too the point. Long, convoluted answers with more detail or information than you asked for is a deceptive indicator.

10. **Overly Polite.** Business is business, and a business meeting should be run like one. If the person is trying hard to be nice and likeable, that's a red flag. For example, midway through your sales appointment, you get a compliment on your clothes or shoes or whatever. What the prospect is actually doing is trying to be more likeable for the purpose of trying to get you to trust and believe him.

11. **Diminishing the Importance of Your Question.** This one is very straightforward; the prospect will say something like, "Why

does that even matter?" or "Why do you ask—is that a big deal?" It's yet another tactic to avoid answering the question and to buy more time to come up with a deceptive answer.

12. **Being on the Offense.** This deceptive indicator is similar to attack mode, but rather than directly attacking you, the prospect will answer with questions designed to put you on the defensive side of the interaction.

   These types of questions are common, and include:

   "How long is this meeting going to take?"
   "Why are you even asking me this?"

13. **Attempting to Narrow a Simple Question.** Here, the prospect gets a fairly simple question from you, but instead of answering directly, he feels trapped, and will try to change the wording or scope of your question. He may also try to diminish the importance of your question.

   The purpose of this deceptive tactic is to avoid answering the full question, and to shrink the scope of what you're asking so the person can worm his way out of it by giving a simple response that doesn't answer your entire question.

14. **Referral Statements.** This is a big one. It's also very powerful and effective, so you need to be on the lookout for these.

   A referral statement is when someone repeats or refers back to something they'd said earlier. You might hear, in reference to a competitor, "As I told the last guy..." or, "As I said previously on the phone..."

   Part of the power of referral statements is repetition. The more you hear something repeated, the more likely you are to believe it. That's why it's so important to watch for these types of statements and be aware of when they're happening. This is a subtle deceptive tactic that many people miss.

15. **Using God or Religion.** You've almost certainly heard people say at one time or another:

    "I swear to God."
    "With God as my witness."

    An extreme example of this might be someone taking a Bible out of his desk and saying, "I am a man of God." In that situation, they're not only making the statement, but also using a prop to dress it up. You can certainly mark this one up as a strong deceptive indicator.

16. **Having a Selective Memory.** You've seen this in courtroom dramas as well as in Congressional hearings and interviews with politicians.

    Perhaps the most famous, albeit old, example of this was Colonel Oliver North testifying before Congress in the late 1980s over the Iran-Contra scandal. Colonel North answered virtually every question with, "I don't recall." You may hear a prospect say, "I don't remember," when you know it's an important matter that he almost definitely knows. "Not to my knowledge," "As far as I know," and similar statements belong in this group.

17. **Truth Qualifiers.** This is when someone uses tactics to either exclude information, avoid answering a question, or the like. However, just one of these does not mean the person isn't being truthful. You want to look out for multiple truth qualifiers. They include:

    "Frankly..."
    "To be perfectly honest..."
    "Basically..."
    "Fundamentally..."

    I know you've already heard some of those, if not all, in sales appointments, so going forward these should really stand out and you'll begin to notice them when prospects say them.

18. **Convincing Statements.** This one is huge, and is perhaps the biggest red flag of all that someone is deceiving you. What the person is attempting to do is convince you that they're being honest and that you should believe them.

    The key here is not getting a direct answer, such as a simple yes or no. Instead, you'll hear things such as:

    > "Our organization would never do that ..."
    > "Ask anyone around here about my reputation ..."
    > "Do you really think I'd jeopardize my job over this?"

    To defeat a convincing statement, simply agree with it! So, if a decision-maker says he'd never jeopardize his job by making a purchase without lots of time for thought and consideration—or to "sleep on it" as the old excuse goes—you come right back with, "Yes, of course I know you'd never jeopardize your job."

    What this communicates to the prospect is that their statement had no impact whatsoever on you.

THE BODY LANGUAGE OF DECEPTION

In addition to verbal cues to listen for, there's deceptive body language to watch for.

Be careful with this. For example, many, if not most, books on body language say that crossed arms while talking are an indication that the person is lying. This is only a half-truth—half because the odds of it being true are about 50/50! Hey, some people feel comfortable standing or sitting that way, and I know I do it quite a lot without even realizing it.

Remember, as with the verbal indicators, you cannot rely on just one. You need multiple indicators in order to confidently conclude that the person you're talking with isn't being entirely truthful.

1. **Covering up mouth or eyes.** This is a common indicator and one you can even see in actual trial court footage on those crime channels. A deceptive witness will unknowingly have his or her hand in front of the mouth rather than in a normal position.

   Likewise, a hand covering eyes to any degree, or even closing of the eyes while talking, is a red flag.

2. **Excessive throat clearing or swallowing.** The classic example of this is someone under pressure, sounding off a big gulp before answering a question. Excessive throat clearing is another indicator. In being powerful, contrary to popular belief, confident people don't use lots of hand gestures when they talk, because hand gestures are considered a sign of release of nervous energy. So are these indicators.

3. **Excessive grooming gestures.** If you ask a prospect a question and he spend a second or two fixing his tie, or cuff links, or tucking in his shirt before answering, that's a deceptive indicator. Be careful with this one though. I once worked with someone who was obsessed with having his shirt tucked in perfectly, military-style, and would endlessly fix it and tuck it in all day long until it could drive you crazy, so use your best judgment here and consider whether other red flags are present or not.

4. **The swiveling chair trick.** If you ever have prospects coming to your office to meet with you, be absolutely sure you have them sit in a swiveling chair, like a typical office desk chair. (You know, like the one in the Oval Office.)

   Once that prospect is seated, observe if and/or how that chair is moving around. If the person is swiveling, or rolling back and forth on the casters, or rocking in it, you have a big red flag that the person is releasing the anxiety that comes from lying through those physical motions.

It's a standard CIA interrogation technique to use swiveling chairs when interrogating subjects.

PUTTING IT ALL TOGETHER

I can't stress this enough: You need more than just one deceptive indicator, and preferably more than two, in order to determine if someone is lying or not. If you get one deceptive indicator, there's a good chance that's it's just a fluke and that's how the person naturally acts. That's why it's so important to keep a tally in your head of how many deceptive indicators you've seen. If you reach three or more, you can be pretty sure you're being lied to.

Oh, and never, ever call the prospect out on his lie! As I said, keep it in your head. When you pick up on a deceptive indicator, make a note of it in your head, then ask some more questions while you continue to watch and listen to your prospect.

Some of the information in this chapter was gleaned from the book *Spy the Lie: Former CIA Officers Teach You How to Detect Deception* (St. Martin's Press, 2012) by Philip Houston, Michael Floyd, and Don Tennant. The information I've given you here is just a tiny fraction of what the authors have to offer, so check it out if you're interested in becoming an expert on detecting lies. Their website is qverity.com.

Sales Badassery Truth

If you can't tell if your prospect is giving legitimate objections or is lying to you, you're flying blind and will be at their mercy.

10

PERSUASION THE SALES BADASSERY WAY

Sales Badasses Never Sell—
They Make People Want to Buy

Remember my definition of selling in a previous chapter? I define selling as an uphill battle of trying to convince a prospect to buy from you when they may not necessarily need or even want what you have to offer.

That's why it's so important not to just qualify prospects, but to disqualify them. Make them earn the right to meet with you; don't be like those naïve rookies who jump in the car to meet with anyone who is willing to see them.

To fully understand this, if you're good at sales, there's a pretty good chance that you may have sold and closed sales with people who may not really have wanted to buy from you.

My friend and fellow author Dave Lakhani, author of *Persuasion: The Art of Getting What You Want* (Wiley, 2005), correctly points out that there is persuasion, and then there is manipulation.

Here are the two terms defined and differentiated, so you understand this concept:

Manipulation: Getting someone to do something specifically for your benefit and not necessarily theirs. For example, using high-pressure sales tactics to get people to buy what they may not really need, just so you can get your commission.

Persuasion: Getting someone to do something for *your mutual benefit*. You win by making a sale and getting paid for it, and the prospect gets something that will benefit them.

See the difference? Manipulation is about selfishness. Manipulators will "cold read" people and then introduce them to the closer who is best suited to their personality type. Likewise, I've seen a famous author running a seminar, which cost thousands of dollars. His next upsell was an even more expensive seminar, and once some people signed up for it, he had the buyers and nonbuyers go to opposite sides of the room, and had the buyers mock the nonbuyers to humiliate them into buying.

That is one of the most insidious forms of manipulation I've ever witnessed, and I personally do not believe that people who operate like that will last for the long term. Instead, people will see them for what they are, and abandon them.

Don't fall into that trap. If you attempt to manipulate prospects into buying, word will get out that you're dishonest, pushy, obnoxious, greedy, and whatever else they throw at you. And while you may not realize it, the business community in most cities is very well connected, so believe me when I say that word will get out if you become a manipulator.

Another example of manipulation I've seen is in the car business. Some automobile dealers have a sales process where they sell based only on the monthly payment. They don't discuss the actual price of the car, and will get someone to agree to a monthly payment they're comfortable with, when in reality the customer may very well be paying over sticker price and not realize it until it's too late. Indeed, when I sold cars, we routinely sold pickup trucks to contractors for as much as $5,000 over the factory sticker price, because as businessmen, they look at cash flow without paying enough attention to whether they're getting a fair deal.

CUSTOMERS ALWAYS COME FIRST

If you're not serving your customers above and beyond their expectations, you won't keep those customers. Someone will come along with lofty promises and a better price and steal them out from under you. That's why customer satisfaction isn't enough. You need raving fans who will sing your praises. (And by singing your praises, I mean sending you tons of referrals and introductions.)

As I was in an email exchange with a colleague today I remembered a prime example of someone who has succeeded greatly by practicing the idea of customers first and that sales prospects take second place in line.

I tell you this story because I read tons of books, and continue to educate myself on sales. Sadly, there are self-proclaimed sales experts who will tell you to answer the phone and reply to emails, first and foremost, to people who haven't yet given you money, and if it's a customer and you already have their money, let them wait.

It doesn't take an Einstein to see why this strategy is business suicide. And it obviously comes from those who are obsessed with gaining new customers, without knowing (probably from lack of real-life experience) that it's not only much easier to sell an existing customer than to gain a new one, but also that gaining a new customers has zero value if you also lost an existing one in the process!

And guess what? Blowing off your paying customers so you can spend all your time going after new ones is either going to leave you unemployed or put you out of business, depending on what position you're in.

In any case, I had purchased a website—a potential business—from a prominent person you've most likely heard of. Despite his marketing genius, he hadn't been able to make it work, so we made a deal in which I'd take ownership and give it a shot while giving him limited marketing access to the site's email list.

The site took a back seat to everything else I've got on my plate; it remained on my web server for a long time just sitting there.

Before I did anything with it, it got down to only three customers. Three. And I was one of them!

Despite that, this person, who sold one business for over $10 million and makes additional millions each year in his other businesses, freaked out during the website move when I changed hosting companies. Inevitably, those sorts of things never go well no matter how much the transition people promise it will, and the site went down.

Correction: One single solitary feature went down.

My colleague dropped everything he was doing and got on me to fix this. I said, "But there are only three customers, and I'm one of them, so that's two – surely they can wait?"

Nope.

It didn't matter that this very successful multimillionaire entrepreneur was rolling in cash and could afford to lose two customers. He *still* refused to lose two customers.

Wait! Another correction: They were now my customers. But since he originally marketed the service to them under *his* name, he wasn't about to have it dragged through the mud.

If a successful multimillionaire will drop everything he's doing, meaning marketing and product development activities that bring in new cash—and this guy goes nonstop—over two customers who aren't even paying him, then I'd accept that as a very good explanation about why he's so highly respected. He gets new book deals for the asking, has an email subscriber list of millions of people who are loyal and keep buying from him, can get on media anytime he wants, and more. All because people who are vying to give him new money get put on hold *so that existing customers can be taken care of first!*

WHAT MOTIVATES YOU TO SELL?

Now it's time for the hard part: To take a good look at yourself and your past sales and determine whether you've used manipulation tactics, either intentionally or unknowingly.

Did you make a lot of sales because you knew your solution would help and benefit those customers? Or did you make a lot of sales *solely* to earn money and get big fat commission checks?

In my experience, most sales professionals fall into the latter category. They're concerned with their income first and foremost. Okay, so they've helped some customers along the line. However, there are just as many who were high-pressured into buying something they really didn't need.

The best sales professionals—and the most successful—do not fall into that category. The top performers are people who make it a priority to actually fulfill a need or solve a problem for the customer, rather than try to force everyone they meet with to buy.

It may sound paradoxical that the people who are more concerned with helping customers than with their own bank account end up being the most successful and the highest earners overall.

It's all about reputation.

As I said, most cities have a close-knit business community. Business owners and leaders all know each other through things like Rotary Clubs, business roundtable groups, chambers of commerce, philanthropic work, church, their kids school, and many other places.

(Sales Badassery Tip: If you can afford it, send your kids to private school. Many states offer vouchers for this purpose. My kids go to private school, and the parents there are hands-down the most powerful networking group I've ever encountered. I'm talking CEOs,

VPs, high-power lawyers, doctors, and the like. If you can swing it, do it, and get to every parent event they offer.)

I live in Dallas, and the metro area is the fourth largest in the United States with a population over eight million. And yet, in Dallas, it seems like every decision-maker knows all the others as well! In fact, I can't get through a day without running into another business owner I know, unless it's one of those days when I go direct from home to office and back home again, though having said that, I still run into everyone I know in the building.

What this all means is that if you manipulate people into buying— if you're screwing people by making your income a priority over their best interests—word will spread very quickly and you're going to be looking for a new career other than sales or moving to a new city where you can start fresh with a clean slate.

So just don't manipulate people. Don't do it. Like that crooked seminar speaker, you'll make more money in the short term, but in the long term, you'll be finished sooner than you realize.

HOW MISGUIDED PERSUASION HURT ME

It's time for another story of one of the many times I screwed up. And by the way, if you get through a sales or business book and the author hasn't told you all of his or her mistakes so you can learn to avoid them, you're not getting the value you expected when you bought that book. Throw it away. Better yet, burn it. Making no mistakes means you've made no success.

A long, long time ago, in a place far, far away (seriously), I was running with my dog and experienced a severe ankle sprain. My foot didn't fully clear a curb and the impact was so severe that the cartilage on the two affected bones banged into each other hard, damaging the cartilage. There was no way for doctors to fix it. To this day there still isn't one. I went to an urgent care, they told me to use the

RICE formula (rest, ice, compression, and elevation) and gave me a prescription for Motrin 800s.

Fast-forward about ten years and it had degenerated into severe end-stage arthritis. I had a minor surgery to buy time, and it bought over eight years. Or I should say, eight painful years. Then I had major surgery—a total ankle replacement. Keep in mind that although the hip is a simple ball-and-socket joint, and the knee is a simple hinge joint, the ankle is a universal joint that must move in all directions. The result is that an ankle replacement has the longest and most complicated surgery out of any of those joint replacements, along with the longest recovery time.

The total cost of the ankle replacement including post-op doctor appointments and medication was well north of $300,000, and I had to pay a good chunk myself thanks to post-Obamacare garbage health insurance.

Thinking I was "fat and happy," I didn't do much. I spent days in bed for two weeks with the foot elevated per doctor's orders, and I'm glad I did because it really worked. I was the only case he'd ever seen with no swelling when the cast came off after more than a month. Then it took a total of about four months to get back to walking seminormally with no boot or brace. Going back to my office felt strange, I'd been laid up at home for so long.

Meanwhile, I'd let my businesses stagnate. I let it stagnate so far that things started to become financially uncomfortable. And that's when I got nervous and broke Gordon Gekko's rule from the movie *Wall Street*: Never make a decision based on emotion.

I started to email offers to my subscriber list a dozen times a day. Literally, I had email queued up every two hours, nonstop, six days a week. (I would always give them a break on Saturday or Sunday.) And it brought in massive amounts of cash! I mean huge! I thought I'd adapted to new times and this was the new plan. I was back at my prior income and loving it.

Wrong.

After several months of this, my subscriber list was burned out. I'd stopped sending content—content that brought endless compliments for my storytelling abilities—persuaded influential people to contact me, and kept my fans captivated and always eager to get the next email. I just hammered them with promotional offers instead. Then after the last person bought, that was it.

Worse yet, sending a dozen emails a day that actually work takes time. I got into the bad habit of working from home instead of from my office because I'd get up and grab my laptop and just start writing email copy. Then before I knew it, it was noon, so I would stay home for the day and keep writing into the evening.

The problem was that although I was burning up my email list, I wasn't planning ahead for when the list would burn out. I knew it would, but I chose to bury my head in the sand and bask in my success at the moment rather than think six months ahead. Think of how many books or how many new courses I could have written in that time, instead of endlessly writing promotional emails that stopped working one day?

So when one of the so-called experts tells you to prioritize your time on getting new business over taking care of existing customers—or in my case, maintain the proper communication to keep them interested in buying again—think about what that advice did to me and the emotional turmoil I went through wondering if I'd be able to keep my kids in private school, if we'd have to move to the suburbs, and so on.

Don't do it. Never make your paid customers second-class citizens. Always prioritize them above and beyond prospective customers. If they gave you their money, you owe them your time and attention.

Now comes the happy-ending version of this story. Being in chronic pain made me a miserable person. I was angry all the time and didn't even realize it. *House, M.D.* is my all-time favorite television show, and now I can understand why. My wife tells me I was literally like House when I was in pain. Indeed, she had to explain the same thing when a good friend's significant other was in chronic pain for some time prior to his own joint replacement; it's just the pain talking and it will pass.

So in the end, although the ordeal—or rather, my own misjudgment —harmed my business for some time, getting out of pain has changed me back into my old self. In fact I've become a lot more empathetic to other people and their own problems and challenges, so, for example, when someone cuts me off in traffic, instead of flipping the bird and thinking that driver is a jerk, I just assume maybe he or she is late for work or is on the way to the emergency room or something similar. In the end I became a better person. I also worry less, having been in the pit already. I value family and people more, and know I can live without money and be happy if I ever had to, not that I plan to. Many people literally cannot be happy without loads of money, and that's sad. Chances are they'll never be happy even with it, because they'll never have enough. Someday they'll be in old age, near death, and wondering why they spent 100% of their lives chasing money instead of actually living life. (But don't get me wrong, I still want piles and piles of money, but I'm simply never going to have any policy other than "family first" and making sure my kids get as much time as possible with me. Most kids don't see their parents enough. Implement and execute what you learn in this book and you'll have a lot more family time too.)

THE LAW OF COMPENSATION

If you have not read Ralph Waldo Emerson's essay on compensation, do it now. You can find it free on the Internet with a quick Google search. Or just buy the book if you prefer, since all of his essays are outstanding.

The Law of Compensation is simple: It states that there are checks and balances all around us, and the most efficient way to achieve success and rise to great heights of achievement is to give first without expectation of anything in return, though in reality, that alone is an effective sales tactic. It makes people feel obligated to reciprocate (by buying from you). It's like when charities mail you a letter with a lifetime supply of return address labels or something else in there that makes you feel obligated to drop a check for some small amount to them in the mail.

Perhaps the best way to explain the Law of Compensation is to give you a real-life example of someone who practiced the opposite in his career, and is now broke and destitute in old age.

We worked together about twenty-two years ago. Everything with him was, "Sure, I'll do it, but I'd better damn well get paid first." And stupid me believed that was the way to go because he was bringing home a nice five-figure commission check each and every month.

Think about this in a job interview: One of the biggest job interview killers is to start asking about salary and benefits and time off during your first interview. All that does is raise a huge red flag to the employer that you're only out for yourself and won't put enough effort into addressing the best interests of the company.

How many times have you heard someone say, "I'm not doing that unless I get paid first!" I see it all the time when I look for good people to whom I can outsource work. If they demand payment in full up front, I move on to the next person. Most will ask for half up front and half upon completion, which to me is fair.

The most successful ones, however, are those who go the extra mile and do the job without demanding payment up front. The best example of that was when I put a website development project out to bid, and while everyone else was sending me price quotes, one developer just did the job without even quoting me first, showed it to me, then told me the cost. Oh, she could have it up and live online on my server in under an hour.

I don't have to tell you who I bought from. That's self-explanatory. And that's the Law of Compensation at work.

One common complaint I hear, particularly in Amazon reviews, is something to the effect of, "All this information is on the author's YouTube channel so this is a complete rip-off when I can get the knowledge free."

What these crybaby losers don't understand is that you rise to prominence by *giving away your best stuff for free*!

The reason this works so effectively is because it accomplishes two important functions. First, it's like a "test drive" for the prospect. They get a nice broad preview of what you have to offer, and that convinces and comforts them about making a decision to buy from you. Second, and more important, it showcases how good you and your offers are!

A great example of this is in the so-called information-marketing business. (I find that a silly name since books represent information for sale, yet no one calls the book business that.)

In that business, which I'm in, authors, experts, and other content providers will flood the Internet with free content to draw people in and get them to the checkout page on their website.

I use an online tool (MeetEdgar) to automate my social media postings. It feeds content to Twitter, Facebook, LinkedIn, and a few others. The last time I looked, I had about 1,200 articles in there that randomly post to social media on a frequent and consistent basis.

Likewise, I know a couple of authors who say they made all their money on YouTube. By shooting a couple of videos a week, or even daily, and continually uploading them to YouTube, they build an audience and gain prominence above and beyond their competitors. One multimillionaire author said that YouTube is the *only* reason he's now wealthy. Think about that.

Here's someone who makes millions a year in the speaking and seminar business, and his entire audience was built by flooding YouTube with so much content that people came flooding in to his sales funnel.

SALES BADASSERY PERSUASION

Let's make one thing clear: We're all in business to make money. That's why I have businesses. That's why you have a business or a job. To make money. And I'm all for it! However, money is only a good thing when it was earned by selling a product or service that truly benefits the customer. Persuasion is built on a strong foundation of trust, honestly, and integrity.

Speaking of which, honesty and integrity are two of the hallmarks of a Sales Badass. I know what you're thinking: The term *Sales Badass* conjures up images of a slick looking, hard-selling rep. In reality, that's how losers operate. Winners are polished and know their stuff, and are also 100% honest and make sure they're helping people and companies and not just pocketing commission checks from sales that were totally unnecessary to the customer.

Here are the keys to effective persuasion that avoids manipulation:

1. Spend Time Only on Qualified Prospects

You've probably noticed by now that I'm not a big fan of qualifying prospects. I instead disqualify them. This will take guts when you start doing it; however, you'll soon find yourself making a significant volume of sales, and you'll do it while spending fewer hours working. (Or if you're all in, double that by working overtime while working smart.)

By disqualifying, what you're looking for are cues that the prospect either cannot financially make the purchase, or isn't really serious about buying right now. A prime example of this was in my phone system days when I'd ask the prospect what their budget was, and was honest and up front that my price would be substantially higher. If they refused to give a budget—and many did because they assumed I'd just price my proposal at their budget limit—I did some quick preliminary math in my head and gave them a ballpark figure. More often than not, they'd recoil at hearing it and get off the phone fast.

What you're doing here isn't trying to get rid of people; you're working to *effectively increase your sales volume exponentially.* Think about it: If 100% of your sales calls were with truly qualified prospects, meaning those who need to buy right now or in the very near future, and who have the financial ability or the credit to make the purchase.

Going back to Frank Bettger's example, by refusing to meet with anyone who hadn't bought by the second appointment, he more than doubled his sales while working less! And when he sat down and did an accounting of the time he was spending on people in appointments—two, three, four, and so on appointments—they were actually taking up more selling time than the qualified buyers did.

It's essential to get the old sales clichés out of your head, things like "fight the good fight," "get out there in the trenches," and so on. These mottos suggest that closing a deal is a fight.

It should never be a fight!

Instead, it should be a mutually beneficial, enjoyable transaction. If you do it right, you'll find prospects actually *asking* to buy rather than you having to close them. (Details on how to do that to come in an upcoming chapter.)

2. Only Meet with the Final Decision-Maker

Even more important than only working with qualified prospects is making sure you're with the final decision-maker.

Tony Parinello, in his book *Selling to VITO (The Very Important Top Officer)* (Adams Media Corp., 1994), explains what a "Seymour" is. A Seymour is someone who always wants to "see more" before making a buying decision.

Or, at least that's what the Seymour wants you to believe. The reality is that all Seymours are non–decision-makers. If they had the power to make a decision and weren't going to buy, they'd just tell you "no" instead of wasting your time and dragging you along because they don't have the courage to say no. Odds are, if you're having your time and efforts wasted by a Seymour, what probably happened is that the real decision-maker already said no, but Seymour doesn't have the courage to break the news to you. (That's why he's Seymour instead of the big boss.)

Some good examples of Seymours you'll encounter are office managers, IT personnel, virtually anyone in middle management, executive assistants, and many, many more. Having said that, sometimes the decision-maker really does delegate the decision and the signing power to a subordinate like an office manager, so you need to be very thorough and detailed in your questioning to find that out. This is common in the medical world; my brother does Web design and backend Web programming primarily for cosmetic surgeons and dentists, and he works almost exclusively with office managers. The surgeons' time is way too valuable for that.

3. Always Be Fully Prepared for Appointments

A common but overlooked mistake by sales professionals is to show up for an appointment without every last thing that could possibly be required.

Think about this: You were just asked to speak at a local Rotary Club last week. What's the first thing you do? Prepare! You create a presentation, you put together slides, and you show up and give an amazing performance.

The same applies to sales appointments. And I'm not just talking about having the proposal and contract with you along with any other documentation you may need in the meeting. I'm talking about researching the company, and researching the key decision-maker(s) you'll be meeting with. LinkedIn makes this super easy on the business and professional side of things, and if you can find their

Facebook and Twitter pages, even better. It's an easy way to get to know what they like personally, find things in common, and find things you can use to gain favor.

For example, the Law of Reciprocity is why charities send out address labels and other freebies. Human nature places the recipient under obligation to reciprocate. For an example of how this applies to sales, imagine you have the name of the person you just set up an appointment with in a few days. You browse his social media profiles and learn that he likes a particular gourmet coffee shop in town, you go pick up a small gift card ($5 or $10 is enough), and you say, "Hey, by the way, I hear you like this place—enjoy a cup on me!"

Using social media to learn the personal interests of your prospect is an extremely powerful tool that few people utilize to its real capability. I post a lot of political things on social media, so a savvy sales professional (if he happens to be of the same political persuasion) will see that and talk politics when he arrives. That'll get me talking, and … BOOM! The salesperson just got me engaged and already liking him because he's singing the praises of something I support.

4. Set Realistic Expectations

Don't overpromise and underdeliver. Heck, for that matter, *never* underdeliver, regardless of what you promised.

I can remember when I was a rookie, making promises I wasn't sure I could deliver on. Telling people what they wanted to hear, rather than the hard truth, definitely got sales, but it was a form of manipulation, not persuasion, and I ended up with some very angry customers who spread the word to other business owners that I screwed them.

Probably the biggest load of shit I told people was unrealistic installation dates. They'd say they needed it installed by next Friday, and I'd say "no problem." I just wanted to get the sale and get out of there. Then, when they got the scheduling call for three weeks later, all hell broke loose. Few customers canceled, but they sure as hell didn't come to me for repeat business, and they told others about what had happened.

There's a school of thought in sales that you should always overpromise then make sure you overdeliver. This is a very risky strategy. What if your overpromise cannot be delivered? If that happens, you've lost repeat business and referrals from that customer and your name will be mud.

I've had someone tell me, "But if you massively overpromise and deliver even only half of that, they're going to be thrilled." No they're not. They were expecting all and you delivered half. You just lost repeat business and referrals! Game over!

After some experience and lots of defeat, I decided to just be totally honest about expectations. And what happened surprised me. When someone said, "We need this installed by next Friday," and I replied with, "Well, the odds of that happening are slim to none. We're on about a three-week installation timeline right now," I fully expected to be shot down the first few times I tried this, but to my amazement, prospects still bought. Indeed, I started closing more deals!

What happened is that when I was telling prospects what they wanted to hear just to get a sale, many sensed this. They saw me as a yes man; a stereotypical Hollywood version of a salesman who is strictly out for himself and not for the best interests of his customers.

When I decided to try—gasp—honesty, prospects appreciated it. When I told them I couldn't meet their deadline and gave them a realistic timeline, they realized they were dealing with a straight shooter, an honest man. Honestly is the best policy, as they say. In this case it built trust between myself and my prospects-turned-customers and they trusted me going forward, gave me repeat business, and kept me busy with fantastic referrals.

Here's the thing: Decision-makers are used to dealing with sales reps who will say anything and will promise the world just to get the sale. When you show up and you don't act like that but, rather, act like a true business professional by being up front about expectations, it's extremely refreshing for them and they'll jump at the opportunity to become your customer. They feel like they're working with the owner of the business and not just another faceless, boring, greedy sales rep.

5. Be Great at Storytelling

Email marketing is a very large part of marketing. I have a lot of high-profile subscribers and several have commented to me, "Your email copy is amazing."

There's really nothing amazing about it, because all I'm doing in those emails is telling stories before asking for the sale at the end.

Remember those so-called pickup artists who make it their obsession to be able to go out and get anyone they want? I mentioned about how they come in under the radar with "I need a female opinion about something" as an opening line.

Once they're in, they ask some silly question that makes the girls laugh, and then they launch into telling stories. Long and very interesting stories. Most of the guys tell true stories, and I know I can certainly think of many funny ones I could tell from my life! Many of them, however, made up fictional stories, which interestingly weren't as effective because when telling about something that actually happened to you, you're a lot more animated and interested in the story versus something that's been made up.

Now here's the kicker: This group's motto was, "Say the same thing to every girl."

In other words, each pickup artist would find the series of stories that worked best, and then stick with those and literally tell the same stories to every woman they met. (Although I can't imagine that would last very long once everyone has heard the same story. Just my two cents on that.)

Why do children, like my beautiful four- and six-year-old daughters, love being told stories? Because stories captivate the human mind! Long before we're supposed to turn into serious adults, the stories stop. And yet novels sell millions upon millions of copies, and the most successful ones turn into movies.

Why? Because human beings love being told stories! So remember, it's not just restricted to children. There is evidence all around you that people love a good story.

6. Never Withhold Bad News

Remember those installation dates I just discussed? Well, even when something was scheduled out a good bit in advance, problems still happened. Installers would call in sick or be on vacation and that'd throw things off.

The loser salesperson—the non-Badass—will avoid the customer and hope someone else on the installation side will call and break the news to them. And they will. However, because it didn't come directly from you, they're going to assume you lied to get the sale.

When you find out there's a delay or some other problem, pick up the phone *immediately* and break the news to your new customer. *And accept responsibility.* When I was still new to sales, or in other words, before I knew any of this, I'd pass the buck. I'd blame it on the technicians or the management or whomever else I could think of. And passing the buck only makes you look bad. You come across as a weasel trying to squirm your way out.

So always tell the truth, and when there's a problem, make sure you are the first person to contact the customer rather than someone in a customer service call center who doesn't know them at all. Don't be afraid, either. By following this, you're going to build a very high level of trust, get repeat business, referrals, and maybe even make a new friend of your customer.

7. If Your Solution Doesn't Truly Benefit the Prospect, Don't Sell It

Remember that buzzword *consultative selling*? It was big for a while, yet in recent years I haven't heard much at all about it.

That's because of something I'm sure you already know. When someone offers a free consultation, what they're really offering is to have a sales appointment. Regardless of what the consultation finds, salespeople—or at least the loser majority of them—will always try to sell the same thing to every customer anyway.

There's nothing "consultative" about that. It's pure deception, plain and simple.

Real consultants don't do that. They don't sell. (Well, except for their consulting services.) I've hired consultants, and they get paid to make truthful recommendations to solve their clients' problems. They may recommend that the client purchase a particular solution, but they're not selling and are not profiting by the sale.

The "free consultation" strategy has been overused for so damn long that prospects know full well that you're not showing up for a consultation, you're showing up to sell them something. You'd have just as much luck trying to run "feel, felt, found" on a prospect!

When I saw this happening, I still used the free consultation offer to get in the door while it still worked. And what did I do? I acted like a real consultant!

I frequently admitted that my solution might not be the best fit for the prospect!

If you want to see a look of true astonishment in a prospect's eyes, say that. (But only if it's true, of course.) Odds are it'll be the first time the prospect has ever even experienced that, and it's a huge breath of fresh air for them to know they're dealing with someone who is ingrained with honesty and integrity.

Two things happen when you do this: First, the prospect has immediate and lasting trust with you and will still want to do business with you regardless. Even if it's not this particular sale, you'll get one from them sooner or later.

Second, and more important, they'll become a raving fan and sing your praises to their peers. And remember, people tend to hang out and socialize with their literal peers, which means decision-makers hang out with other decision-makers. Remember how I explained that most cities have a tight-knit business community? That's why.

The referrals will come *pouring* in.

MAKING HONEST PERSUASION YOUR FOUNDATION

Now that you've seen some specific examples of persuasion over manipulation, you can see there's a common pattern of honesty and integrity in everything the Sales Badass does. And that's what makes someone a Sales Badass. They don't take any crap or disrespect from people, they never waste time on prospects that haven't passed the qualifying-out test, and they make sure their customers get taken care of.

Intent is what separates persuasion from manipulation. Manipulators intend to enrich themselves regardless of the customer's needs, whereas the persuaders are intent on creating win-win situations that benefit all parties involved.

Remember all that information about subcommunication, the nonverbal cues we send out? Human beings have an innate lie detector. It's nowhere near as reliable as watching for the red flags I explained in the chapter on lies, but everyone's subconscious mind watches for cues and creates that "gut instinct" in people about whether they like you.

Regardless of whether our subcommunication is somewhere around 60%, or as high as 93% according to a UCLA study, the fact remains that our body language and how we say things is far more important than what we say.

When you attempt to manipulate someone, red flags go off in their mind and they have a gut instinct not to do business with you. That's because your subcommunication is very much dependent on your intent and your mindset. If you're there to manipulate your way into a sale, it's going to come across. Likewise, if you're there to truly help and benefit the prospect, their gut instinct is going to be positive and they'll be open to you.

When you come from a foundation of honesty and integrity, your subcommunication will show confidence, respect, trust, and many more positive attributes. The longer you practice this, the more ingrained in you it becomes, and the faster and more abundantly your prosperity will come.

Sales Badassery Truth

Only losers overpromise things they can't deliver. The Sales Badass always tells the truth and sets realistic expectations. That builds a very high level of trust and the introductions and referrals that come as a result will exponentially increase your sales success.

11

How to Become a Prominent Sales Badass

It Doesn't Matter Who You Know— What Matters Is Who Knows You

As the old saying goes, "It's who you know that matters."

Although it's true that you will become a composite of the group of people you associate with the most (meaning drop your loser friends and stop loaning them money), it's only a half-truth, if even that, that who you know matters most.

That was true during the Industrial Age, but not now, not in the Information Age.

Heck, even *before* the Industrial Age it was true. (Just not after.) Back in the Agrarian Age—the 1800s and prior—when farming and agriculture were the largest and most dominant industries in the world, you had to get connected to sell your goods.

Think about it: There was no Internet, no phones, the mail took weeks if it was sent a long distance, and the only advertising media available were newspaper ads and flyers, along with cold calls. Back then, cold calls actually worked because there were so few of them and people had far more time on their hands to talk to salespeople than today.

Then along came the Industrial Age. Now depending on whom you listen to, you'll get varying dates on when cold calling died. Jeffrey Gitomer says it hasn't worked since the 1980s. Dan Kennedy says it stopped working in the 1950s. Either way, even decades ago, busy decision-makers got fed up with having their very busy schedules interrupted with cold callers.

As a result, the big thing became connections. You had to get connected. You had to get in with the "old boys' club" in your city. You had to join the right country club or the right church or the right service club, like Rotary or Kiwanis.

The Internet was in its very infancy when I started in sales, so in addition to cold calling, I did what I could to get connected. Today, now that I'm really well connected, I look back on my efforts back then and laugh. When I decided to launch a new business locally in 2012, all I did was go to networking groups—a breakfast group, a lunch group, a happy-hour group (with no alcoholic drinks, to keep a clear head). Yes, that's a lot of time, and, yes, it paid off. Within a year I was pocketing about $20,000 a month in clear profit from that business, all because of networking.

It made my sales-rookie networking strategy of showing up at a group a few times a month look really pathetic by contrast. And, in fact, I'm about to do it again. My wife and kids just left for three and a half weeks to visit her family in New York State so I'm bored—what better way to fill up my time? Well, besides writing this for you …

I'll get into specific detail on my networking secrets in the chapter on the sales badassery networking strategy. (Hint: It wasn't about meeting people at random, it was meeting people with leverage who could bring me ten deals instead of just buying personally.)

Fast-forward to today: How did you get this book?

I didn't make a cold call and interrupt you during your busy day and ask you to buy it. I didn't meet you at a networking event to sell you a book. I didn't speak at a Rotary Club to sell you a book from a table in the back of the room (although I do that and you should too, book or no book).

No. You *found* this book. And you found it because both my publisher and I *positioned* it to get found. And get purchased.

BECOMING PROMINENT IN THE TWENTY-FIRST CENTURY

Back in 2003, when I started my sales training business, I knew it would be smart to trademark my product and my book names, so I got online and went looking for a trademark attorney who could get that done for me.

Hold on, I'm getting ahead of myself. What really happened is that I went online looking for information on how to apply for a trademark. I didn't understand at the time that trademark law is needlessly complex and convoluted and that I'd be better off letting a professional handle it. Besides, my time was worth far more actually working on my business and building an audience versus shuffling paper while trying to avoid all the pitfalls. I would have spent endless hours doing research when that time is better spent generating revenue, which is an important point to remember in all your activities: Is what you're doing going to generate revenue or is it something you should let a professional handle?

What I found was a very thorough, informational website about all things trademark. I read lots of articles and PDFs about what's required to qualify for a trademark, how to apply, all the things that could go wrong, and so on.

Here's the catch: I wasn't reading this on About.com or on Wikipedia. I just happened to be on a local trademark attorney's personal website! By personal I mean it was separate from the firm he worked for.

And I say *happened* although there was no happenstance about it. He knew very well that he was putting together a marketing masterpiece with that kind of knowledge-base site—always remember that content is king, hence why that barrage of promotional-only emails backfired on me—and that site got him lots of new clients, including my company. And he optimized that website to show up in local search so I'd find it in my particular city.

Needless to say, I hired him, and stuck with him a while even when he changed law firms—or at least until he changed once too many times, at which time I moved everything to a local trademark attorney I'm friends with.

THE WORLD WON'T BEAT A PATH TO YOUR DOOR

If a man can write a better book, preach a better sermon or make a better mouse trap than his neighbors, though he builds his house in the woods, the world will make a beaten path to his door.

—*Ralph Waldo Emerson*

Even when the Sage of New Hampshire, as Emerson was known, wrote that, how on earth can anyone make a beaten path to a man's door if they don't know about that man?

Does the man build a better mouse trap and hope the screams of dying mice will attract buyers of mouse traps? (Hint: When I had a rodent problem once, I just started putting cat food outside, and the dirty little critters disappeared within a week. And I had a group of cats hanging around always waiting for me to come home, which was fun at a time when I was in between dogs.)

If you write the ultimate Great American Novel and then hole up with it in your house in the woods, do you honestly believe that you're going to be the next Stephen King or J. K. Rowling? *How is anyone going to buy a copy of that book if they don't know about it or about you?*

Emerson's famous quote may have had some grain of truth to it a hundred and fifty years ago, but today, it's one of the very worst pieces of business advice you can take.

Or is it? The good news is that unlike J. K. Rowling, you don't have to chase and pursue to get what you want. She had to rely on getting signed with a publisher to get what she wanted.

Count your blessings that you live in the Information Age, that you have the Internet at your disposal, because with each successive year, the possibilities and capabilities it brings you to make yourself known to that segment of your market who are predisposed to buy from you increases exponentially.

As I outlined this book, it was like a huge wake-up call that things have changed so much since my most recent book, *The Never Cold Call Again Online Playbook: The Definitive Guide to Internet Marketing Success* (Wiley, 2010).

It's like looking in the mirror each morning as we shave or apply makeup. We see the same face we did the day before, causing us not to realize how much we've aged.

And even when we do, what do we say to ourselves then? "Didn't I look young?" It's amazing to me how much humans will hide their heads in the sand and avoid facing reality head on; it's no wonder that so many needlessly live in financial struggle for their entire lives.

Similarly, that previous book covered things like Google Ad-Words, article marketing, getting active in online forums, using free classified such as Craigslist, and … that's about it. Don't get me wrong—people still buy and rave about the book today because of the information on setting up a website to convert visitors into hot leads, on how to use your web presence to make "back-end" money, on using it to generate offline income, and so much more.

But those methods of getting people to notice you in the first place? Google AdWords now returns paper-thin profit margins, and only after burning through tens of thousands of dollars to get it right, excluding many ambitious people trying to start out. My own digital marketing agency won't even take on clients who want to start with AdWords—we only take on existing users. That's how competitive it's become.

Craigslist now charges for a business classified ad; there are so many Internet forums now and they're so crowded that they alone have become a full-time job, and on and on.

So let's move on to what works right now, keeping in mind that by the time this book is in your hands (or on your Kindle) there will already be new ways and means of using the Internet to make yourself known to that most valuable slice of your market.

PODCASTING: TODAY'S MAINSTREAM RADIO

In my last book, I wrote, "Most people I speak with have no idea what podcasting is."

Today, who *doesn't* know what podcasting is? And this change occurred in under a decade! It's because, back then, the iPhone had only been available for three years. Now it's the number-one *best-selling individual product in the world.*

Think about that: Steve Jobs had a life goal of "making a ding in the universe." I'd say he pulled it off by thinking, in his own mind, of something that would eventually become the best-selling single product in the entire world. Do you still doubt Napoleon Hill's statement that "thoughts are things"?

My point is that it's the iPhone that made the change. I remember what a hassle it was to listen to or watch podcasts on my computer. Now I open the Podcasts app and not only are all the latest episodes of the podcasts I subscribe to downloaded and waiting for me, I can view their entire episode list and even have recommended podcasts shown to me. Better yet, I can avoid wasting time in the car by listening to music, yet don't have to listen to just a small piece of an audiobook in the time I can listen to a complete podcast episode—depending on the specific podcast, of course.

In other words, back when I was a kid, we all had our pocket FM radios and headphones. Now everyone has a smartphone and earbuds. (For the record, I still use headphones. I really hate earbuds.) In other words, podcasts are the new radio.

Here's the better news: Podcasting has become stupid easy to get started with. I remember in 2007, when my company purchased an $8,000 video camera just to have full HD, because in 2007, high-definition video was a big deal and just having "HD" in the podcast title attracted viewers. (That camera is now worth only a few hundred dollars.) Today, HD is the norm. Or I should say, HD as it was known in 2007 *was* the norm—with 1,920 horizontal pixels per line. Now, it is completely obsolete with 4K and 5K television sets becoming the norm. In fact, if I tried to watch my old television from 2007, it'd probably look like standard definition to me now.

And that's what happened with podcasting. A podcast went from a rare thing that took some considerable investment and effort to start up, mostly with poor quality as a result, to something that anyone can do with nothing more than a smartphone. And I literally mean a smartphone and nothing else. It's not the optimal method for audio quality but it works, and if you already have it, consider podcasting free for you. (And one of those 15-dollar tripods will help, too.)

Consider these current statistics:

- 44% of Americans have listened to a podcast.
- 26% of Americans regularly listen to podcasts monthly.
- One-third of Americans ages 25 to 54 listen to multiple podcasts monthly.
- There are approximately 48 million people listening to podcasts regularly, and that number goes up by about 6 million every year.
- The average listener consumes five podcasts per week.

- 49% of podcasts are listened to at home or work, and 22% in the car while driving.
- Listeners listen to 40% more shows than last year (and this also goes up every year).
- And here's the biggest one of all: 80% of listeners listen to *each and every episode* they subscribe to, and they listen to an average of seven per week.
  (Source: Edison Research survey)

Getting Started

Now let's get on with what you'll need to produce a quality podcast:

1. **Microphone.** I do have a professional microphone set up in an area I arranged specifically for podcasting and recording; however, in all honesty an inexpensive USB headset works just as well. Unless your listener is in a very-high-end car or at home with an audiophile sound system, they won't be able to tell the difference anyway. (The sound system on my most recent Mercedes-Benz was a $7,500 option, and worth every penny, just so you understand the possibilities.)

   You can grab a good one for under 20 bucks on Amazon or at any local electronics or office supply store. (Amazon hint: Read reviews, but first go to the full reviews page and search for the words "paid" or "exchange." If you see multiple reviews starting or ending with a disclaimer to the effect of, "I posted this honest review in exchange for receiving a free sample of the product," then there's nothing honest about that review or that seller—move on.)

2. **Audio Gear.** This is entirely optional and all of this can be done with software, but I like gadgetry—all men do—so I use the hardware versions. And besides, they won't crash or lock up. The three to look for, whether hardware or software, are:

a. **De-Esser.** This removes excessive "sss" noises that we all inadvertently make while speaking. It gets annoying and tiring for a listener, so it's best to remove them.

b. **Compressor.** What this does is keep your voice at a constant audio level, within reason; if you need to shout or yell for effect, it'll still come through, or you can dial the knob down a bit. (See how fun gadgetry is?) What the compressor does is ensure that whether your voice is getting tired and your volume drops, or if you don't stay at the exact distance from the microphone the entire time (which is nearly impossible unless you're using a headset), the listener will hear the same audio level. Even if you're using a USB headset as I recommend, your voice will still get tired, or your voice may be weak some days, so use it.

c. **Gate.** While the compressor takes care of your voice level, the gate keeps background and extraneous noises out. For example, my private office has a lovely freeway view. (Hey, I can handle distractions, but most podcast listeners will not want to hear background noise in podcasts.) It's not terribly loud but a passing fire truck with sirens blaring will naturally be heard, so the gate keeps it out. Be aware that with a gate, if you whisper or add something else very low-volume for effect, it may very well get cut off by the gate, so adjust the effect level appropriately.

3. **Software.** If you have a Mac, it comes with GarageBand, so you're good to go. Even with a Mac, I like Adobe Audition, and pay around $20/month for it through Adobe Creative Cloud. I also keep a voice recorder around so if I get an idea that I want to record right then and there, I can use it. My iPhone works well for that too, just with slightly lower audio quality. There are endless options and information available online, so I'll leave that to you.

4. **A Computer.** I already know you have this, so fire it up, search for how to add a podcast to iTunes on Apple's help site, and you're good to go!

Creating Your Content

Whenever I talk about content, remember that not only is content king, always think back to my story of how I profited nicely but *only in the short term* by pummeling my subscribers with promotional emails only and no content. The gravy train ended faster than I could write those promo emails.

No one wants to hear, "Buy! Buy! Buy! Sale! Half-Off! Limited Time!"

What they want to hear is something interesting. Something that will help them, whether it's in their relationships, in their job, at their business, with their hobbies, with their golf game, you name it. If it's interesting to your target market, they will be engaged, listen to, and follow you.

What just happened there? I said they would follow you. That just made you the leader. You're in charge. And remember who wins every sale? That's right, whomever is in charge. That's you—you're the boss!

Now that I'm back to content, my subscriber list is engaged and buying again. And I'm the boss again.

Also think back to that trademark lawyer, and how having content – and nothing but content—won me as a new client.

People ask me how I can write books. When I explain that it's no sweat because I'm writing nonfiction books based upon my very own experience and knowledge. I'm simply telling you what I know. That's all there is to it. It's nowhere near the difficult task of writing a fictional book and creating characters, plot, and all that. I'm simply writing from my own life experience and what has worked flawlessly for both myself, as well as for salespeople I've trained or coached.

Once I explain that and say, "Just do it," usually they still say, "I still couldn't do it." And they're right. As Henry Ford said, whether you think you can do something or not, you're right. They defeat themselves before they even begin. Correction: They never intended even to get started.

So what do you know that interests your market? Don't tell me "nothing," because if that were true, you'd already be out of your market, either willingly or not, and you or your employer would be out of business. (I speak from experience —I'd been in a sales position selling something nobody cares about in the telecom space, and they're long out of business.) In fact, your day-to-day activities are your best sources of your content—namely, your prospects' and customers' problems.

Solve a problem for someone and you'll be his or her hero for life. I've been told that tons of times when meeting someone in a business environment: "Oh wow, Frank Rumbauskas, you're my hero!" The first couple of times I asked people why, I expected them to say they made millions using my books, and some have; however, it's usually something simple. They'll tell me I saved their jobs and now they're in major markets making several hundred thousand a year. Or that they're able to work less and can finally spend the time that their kids needed with them, and they sleep better at night because of it.

That reminds me of a Sales Badassery Tip: as the Godfather said, "A real man spends time with his family." I don't care if you're a man or a woman; what matters is that you use this book and the strategies in it to have more free time to spend with your family. I've had people tell me they spend an hour in the morning having breakfast with their kids, or 45 minutes after work, and they think that's good enough. As a parent who spends an enormous amount of time with my children compared with most people, I can tell you that they need as much of your time as you can possibly give them.

If you're single or otherwise childfree, work your ass off! Use the time you have now to put in those 12-hour days, or to spend weekends wining and dining big whale prospects. (Hey, I've done it plenty of times.)

Okay, back on point: To get warmed up, so to speak, listen to other podcasts relevant to your market or your industry. Read articles and get on YouTube and watch videos. This will give you tons of ideas for a framework that your content can take. Although you absolutely should not copy anything verbatim (unless of course you like being on the receiving end of lawsuits), I'll quote that trademark lawyer who said, "Ideas cannot be copyrighted." Remember that 99.9% of what you read or will read in any nonfiction sales or business book is not new. It's just that some of us are better at explaining it than others. If you don't believe me, check out Amazon reviews. Go to the one- and two-star reviews on any sales or business book and you'll see a bunch of loser crybabies posting, "I could've gotten this information free on the Internet."

Sure they could. But those negative reviewers are losers who aren't putting in the time and effort to succeed anyway, so what's the use?

The other thing to remember is actually an eye-opening statistic: The majority of Fortune 500 CEOs read about one new book per week. US presidents generally do the same. (I don't know how they have the time when they sleep as little as four hours per night … or maybe that isn't actually true?)

What does that tell you? *Successful people read books.* A lot. You're doing it right now, so congratulations! You're ahead of the 98% or so of people who, when they ask me how they can become me, first I tell them they can't and they need their own message. Then I recommend a specific book that will answer their questions. If it's just general success, I tell them to read *Think and Grow Rich* by Napoleon Hill as a starting point, and to read it three times and then we can discuss it. Invariably they whine—so much so that I've come to expect it—that they don't like to read, don't have time to read, and every other excuse in the book. (No pun intended.) Gee, no wonder they're not successful yet! See, I said the word *yet*. I told you I have more faith in humanity after my own personal struggles. (Maybe.)

On that same note, this concept will remain true throughout the rest of this chapter. I'm not going to revisit content creation; there are hundreds of books and courses on the topic, and tens of thousands of articles and guides online. Since it's a topic that takes an entire book to cover, I'll spare you the details and avoid doubling the size of this one! I mean, seriously, would you even have picked this up if it were double in length?

Finally, on that note, remember that brevity is important. I can turn on a microphone and talk for three hours when the average listener prefers podcasts that last less than 16 minutes. So, plan on making yours 15 minutes. Once you build a large audience, you can start making them longer, but keep in mind the average US commute time is 25 minutes and a disproportionate number of listeners listen while driving to and from work. I guess I'm lucky since sales professionals are in the car a whole lot more than that …

DOMINATE YOUR SPACE WITH YOUTUBE

Everyone knows that Google is the world's largest search engine. Okay, maybe not someone's great-grandparents (my kids have three; longevity thrives on both sides of my family, so they're very fortunate).

However, when I ask someone to guess what the number-two search engine in the world is, they usually say Bing or Yahoo. *Wrong*! The second-largest search engine in the world is YouTube.

Think about that for a moment. People spend hundreds, even thousands, of hours doing Search Engine Optimization (SEO), something I do not recommend, and spending tens of thousands each month on Google AdWords to get the ads on top of the page to generate clicks. Meanwhile, YouTube is relatively easy to get people watching your videos.

Again, as with podcasting, if you have a smartphone, you're good to go. You can even upload a video to YouTube right from your phone—no computers involved.

If you want to get advanced, you can get a lapel microphone that clips onto your shirt or jacket. I used to use wireless ones but got tired of changing batteries, so I just run the cable from me to the camera (or a phone if that's what you're using) and the problem is solved.

When it comes to content, I've explained that in detail. Indeed, you can even use your podcasts and recycle them as videos. Simply do a "talking head" video with just you talking about the main points of the podcast. With smartphones capable of recording in HD now, and YouTube supporting HD, you can create a very professional-looking video with just your smartphone.

In my case, what I do is take articles, especially the ones that have proven most effective when sent as marketing emails, pay an outsourcer I found on Upwork to turn it into a stunning, beautiful PowerPoint, then I do a voiceover on it and export it as a video. Upload it to YouTube and then it's done.

Similarly, I frequently read those articles aloud and do a talking head video. I keep a dress shirt and suit jacket in my office so I can throw them on at any time and look good when recording.

Volume and Frequency Are Key to YouTube

Here's the catch, because there's always a catch: If you want YouTube to work for you, you cannot go and upload a dozen or so videos and wait for people to start contacting you. It takes a lot to get noticed. That's why it's important for you to carve out a regular time slot on a regular basis to create a video. I don't care if it's weekly, twice a week, or even daily.

In Grant Cardone's book *The 10X Rule: The Only Difference Between Success and Failure* (Wiley, 2011), he explains that no matter what you plan, think you need to do, or what you project, it will always take ten times the effort you thought it would.

In other words, if someone thinks it will take X dollars to get a project done, most likely it'll cost ten times that amount. If you think it'll take two prominent connections in your city to build a strong network, make it 20.

If you doubt this, I can tell you from real-life experience that it's true. When I launched my consulting practice—which wasn't so much a launch as me deciding to just do it—it took more than 10 times the effort, contacts, follow-up calls, personal visits, direct mail, and more, than I had any idea that it would. I assumed my 10% effort would work. It didn't. I really had to kill it and hit it hard. I had to go "all in," as they say. And you need to do the same thing when it comes to creating content if you want to become a prominent Sales Badass.

I'm not saying you need to create 10 videos a day. I know I don't have time for that. However, when it comes to content, quantity is just as important as quality. The more videos you produce and upload to YouTube, the larger your channel will grow and the more subscribers and eventual buyers you will get.

Getting Your Videos Watched

If you just upload videos to YouTube and do nothing else, you'll actually get some results if you do enough of them and the content is of decent quality.

However, to really blow things up and dominate, if you can get a surge of people to click on your video link all within a short period of time, that video will skyrocket in YouTube rankings and that means it's going to show up on a lot more screens as users browse YouTube.

The thing to do is send it out to your email subscriber list. That way everyone gets the email at the same time and enough views occur in that short time that the video gets a lot more exposure to YouTube users who don't know about you yet, and that's just the point—to draw them in, get them interested, and get them into your funnel.

As a side note, remember what I said about the time I hammered my subscribers with promotional emails only? That's right; it was a disaster. So don't do it in your videos. Remember, content is king, and the video is a way to simply get the prospect to know you exist and that you're an authority in your industry. (This tends to happen automatically if you put enough quality content out there.)

I won't go into building an email list here. That's covered in *The Never Cold Call Again Online Playbook: The Definitive Guide to Internet Marketing Success* (Wiley, 2010).

If you have an email list, even a small one—my experience is that very small but targeted lists outproduce huge lists—then every time you create a video, send the link out in an email to all of your "tribe," so to speak. That way, they'll generally watch the video within a small timeframe, say one day, and that will help your video rank both on YouTube and on Google itself. (Notice how video results frequently show up at the top of Google when you search for something.)

Your Video's Description

This is key to getting your video to rank well in both YouTube and Google. The trick is to transcribe the entire video and then use that transcription as the video description. I'm serious—literally cut and paste the entire transcription into the description part of the video.

What this does is populate the video's page with relevant phrases and keywords that will cause your video to show in search results when someone is searching either on Google or on YouTube for something relevant to you.

You can have this done for five bucks on Fiverr.com or you can use software such as Dragon Dictate to get it done. Either way, this is key to creating a successful video that will rank well, especially after your tribe all watches it and it gets a lot of views in a short time. Having that amount of content in the video description is like slapping a supercharger on that. It gives the video the extra boost it needs to do well.

Concerning keywords, my best suggestion is to search online for a keyword suggestion tool, and use one of the many free ones that show up in Google search. Paste your video description—the transcription—into the tool, click the button, and it will spit out a list of relevant keywords. Use those in the keywords section of the video.

LIVE VIDEO

Live video is closely related to YouTube videos—and remember, there are dozens of video platforms you can upload to; however, YouTube is the king and if you use YouTube and only YouTube you'll still be miles ahead of the rest of the pack.

Live video is popular because it's more engaging for people than recorded video. They know they're watching you literally as the words are coming out of your mouth. Even try going unscripted. Most of my very best content was the result of just sitting down and writing, or turning on the video camera and talking, without really knowing what I'd be talking about. Whatever came to mind, that's what I went with.

Here are some of the many places you can stream live video. Remember that there's something new seemingly every day, so do your own research and don't limit yourself to this list; there may be something better by the time you read this book:

- **Periscope.** Periscope is the most popular live video streaming app. Sign up for free—it's only available as a smartphone app for iPhone or Android—and you're good to go. Announce your Periscope channel and send the link to your "tribe," whether that's your customer base, your list of prospects you're currently working, your email list, or whatever. And the beautiful part about it is that you can simply grab your phone, open the app, and start streaming! Make things interesting and you'll build a following and have people watching and listening whenever you go live.

- **Facebook Live.** Facebook has also introduced live streaming video, and again, it's as simple as opening an app and start to record. The beauty of this is that, chances are, you already have a substantial number of Facebook friends and hopefully you have followers on your Facebook business page (previously known as a fan page). When you fire up the app, your connections will see it either in their news feed (if you can even call it that with Facebook promoting fake news these days) and it'll also show up in the "Stories" section of the page on the upper right-hand side, keeping in mind that it may have moved by the time you are reading this.
- **Twitter.** Twitter also offers live video streaming. Again, the process is the same and it's via their smartphone app.

TIP: To engage viewers, give them an email address to send questions or comments and monitor it as you're streaming. It's the modern-day equivalent of calling in to a radio show.

Live Car Video

This is something that's really caught on fire recently. It's shooting a video while you're driving, whether that video is being recorded for upload later, or whether you're doing it live. (Just don't do the email thing for questions and comments—driving while recording is challenging enough to do safely.)

The process is simple: First, get a smartphone windshield mount. I use the Ram Mount, because it works well for recording along with the speed trap countermeasure apps I use, and the thing is rock solid. It's not the cheapest on the market but it won't move or bounce around as you drive.

Then just do your thing. I personally don't know what's so captivating about watching people drive. A lot of people who've done well for themselves do it just to show off their Bentley or whatever. (That's called Sales Douchebaggery, not Sales Badassery.) Others, like me, do it only because they know people love it. And I do a lot of thinking on the road so it's a great time to let my thoughts run free and get them recorded, or live streamed; it doesn't matter how it gets to people with the ability to buy from me, as long as it gets to them.

And even if viewers aren't buyers, putting out enough video content builds buzz and word-of-mouth, which is exactly what made my first book a *New York Times* best-seller. It was a simple matter of hammering the world with content nonstop. When I launched that book, mega best-seller Ann Coulter launched a book on the same exact day, and despite her around-the-clock cable news coverage, I kept her at number two on Amazon all week. All because of word-of-mouth building buzz about the book.

Sales Badassery Tip: A teleprompter makes shooting video much easier, particularly when it comes to repurposing an article as a video. It's not always easy just to memorize the whole thing. Here's the thing: Teleprompters are very expensive, but there's a workaround. I found an iPad teleprompter setup that allows you to put in an iPad with the text in it and a teleprompter app fired up, and the text moves along as you speak so you don't have to worry about having someone to scroll it for you. The kit that uses an iPad to make a teleprompter is relatively inexpensive, and for the iPad, I use the ancient, original iPad that was our very first. If you don't have an old one lying around, you can get one for next to nothing on eBay. (And probably an iPad teleprompter rig, too.)

LINKEDIN

LinkedIn, in my opinion, is the ultimate business networking venue in the world. Notice I didn't say it's the best social media site, or the best networking site. I said *it is the best networking venue* in the world.

Of all my sales training products, my LinkedIn training courses are perennial best-sellers for us.

Consider the fact that nearly half of all millionaires are on LinkedIn, that virtually every Fortune 1000 executive is on LinkedIn, the average CEO has 930 connections (which means they're accessible to you), over one million professionals have posted articles on LinkedIn, and I could go on and on. It's also one of the best places to look for a better job, by the way. At any given time there are about three million active job openings on LinkedIn.

Finding Your Prime Prospects

What I like to use in looking for new prospective consulting clients is LinkedIn's advanced search. Now for the bad news: LinkedIn took that away from its regular platform. If you want to access it now, you need to pay for LinkedIn Sales Navigator. I think it's around a hundred bucks a month, but well worth it for the level of access you get with it.

The trick is to put the exact description of your ideal customer into the search tool. Be sure to limit by geographic area, otherwise you'll get worldwide results. Once you complete that and click "search," what you're going to see is a list of prime prospects you need to be working.

Now for the big secret: Contacting people on LinkedIn, attempting to get their attention and get in front of them in a sales appointment, is a complete waste of time. It doesn't matter if you can message them because they're a second-level connection, or if you're both in the same group, or if you use an InMail credit. LinkedIn has become so overrun with people sending spammy messages that I don't even check my LinkedIn inbox anymore. I have an assistant do it and most days I get about a hundred messages from people trying to sell me something. Rarely is there a legitimate message in there.

There are many third-party tools available, mostly as plug-ins for Google's Chrome browser. I use one called Lusha. What they do is allow you to visit someone's LinkedIn profile, which you can do in Sales Navigator once you find your ideal search parameters, and the plug-in will pull their contact information that's in their LinkedIn account.

I use it all the time for getting private contact info for potential consulting or sales training clients. Usually when I decide this is a good prospect and I want to start the process of converting them into a client, I'll click on the Lusha button and almost always get a work phone number, a mobile phone number, and both personal and work emails. The nice thing about it is that it lets you preview what information is available, so you can pass on profiles that aren't fully populated with everything you need instead of wasting a credit on them only to find nothing. (Most profiles have everything, though.)

Guess what—people tend to pay more attention and more frequently check their personal email over their work email! Better still, if you email after hours, there's a good chance they'll get the message. You can even schedule emails, depending on which email client you use, to go out when they're at home and checking their personal email.

One tactic I use is to sign up with one of the many sales automation platforms out there that integrate with Gmail or Outlook. That way, you can build a list, or a database, of contact information you've compiled using a tool such as Lusha or even directly from LinkedIn itself.

(Hint: If you export all your contacts, their email addresses will be included in the export and now you have their email addresses, which is especially powerful since something like 90% of LinkedIn users use their personal emails, not their work ones.)

You can use MixMax, ActiveCampaign, or any of the more than dozen out there that are very inexpensive. Add your contacts, create the follow-up emails, set up a schedule for them, then press "go." Some of these tools include a CRM (customer relation management software) so you or someone else can get pinged when it's time to make a phone call or drop something in the mail. You'll also receive notifications if you desire on your smartphone, via email, or in the app itself. You'll know the exact time someone read an email, how many times they forwarded it, how many unique views it got from different people, and so on.

It's nice to call someone 30 minutes after they opened my email. I'm still on their mind but I'm not making it blatantly obvious that I'm playing Big Brother with them and knowing that I received a notification the very instant they opened that email.

Powerful stuff, eh?

LinkedIn Pulse

LinkedIn Pulse is their publishing platform, and until just a couple of years ago you had to be a Mark Cuban or other big-name influencer to get publishing privileges. That's all changed now and any LinkedIn member can post articles on LinkedIn Pulse.

This is huge. The audience on LinkedIn contains very high-powered people. Influencers. And if you can manage to get an article featured, which does occasionally happen, the results can be astronomical.

I recently posted an article. I sent it out to my email subscriber list and it got the usual number of views; however, someone at LinkedIn noticed it and featured it.

It immediately went to the front page of LinkedIn pulse and got over 24,000 views just that one day alone. The sheer volume of those people who visited my website resulted in 800 new email signups and about $10,000—all in one day, because of a LinkedIn Pulse article!

Like all content, quantity is just as important as quality. The more you post, the more you will get noticed and the more people will read your articles, decide that you're someone who knows what you're talking about, and contact you via the bio at the end of your article, or through LinkedIn directly. So once you start publishing, keep an eye on your LinkedIn messages and check them daily.

Likewise, when working with a prospective prospect, you can send them links to your best LinkedIn Pulse articles, especially the ones with a large number of views. What this does is differentiate you from the rest of the crowd who aren't doing these things, and don't worry, 98% of people don't. Even the ones who read books like this put them down and never implement anything. Be one of that 2% of winners who do it. Get it done!

In the bio you'll want to use at the end of each article, include all relevant information necessary for a prospective customer to be able to contact you. It can be your email address, cell number, website link, and so on. And of course, remember that you're both on LinkedIn so they can contact you that way as well.

FACEBOOK AND TWITTER

Although I like Facebook for business purposes, its effectiveness is just a fraction of that of LinkedIn. As Jeffrey Gitomer once told me, "My 10,000 LinkedIn connections are far more valuable than my over 100,000 Facebook likes."

Seriously, how does a "like" generate you any money? I've been in this business for over 15 years and to this day I still cannot trace any money back to Facebook likes.

Likewise, there is zero correlation whatsoever between how many Facebook fans I accumulate and my revenue. In other words, although people may "like" me on Facebook, that doesn't make them buyers.

Here's the problem with Facebook, and this is true with Twitter as well: Less than 1%—yes, I said *less than 1%*—of users on Facebook and Twitter are actively engaged and sharing content.

When you look at how Facebook and Twitter work, the entire point is to make content go viral—to get people sharing it on their own news feeds. So if less than 1%, or in other words, practically no one is sharing your content, what's the point?

MeetEdgar, the automated tool I use to schedule my social media posts, does indeed post regularly to both my Facebook personal page as well as to my various business pages. And lots of people like them and some comment, either good or bad, but virtually no one shares them.

Do they create sales and revenue? Not that I've been able to measure. To this day I still cannot trace one single solitary dollar to Facebook, yet I can trace hundreds of thousands, if not more, to LinkedIn and YouTube.

Does that mean you shouldn't be active on Facebook? It depends. If by "be active" you mean spending a lot of time posting on Facebook and replying to comments, then no.

If it means uploading all your content to the posting tool I use or to many like it, and including your Facebook account along with any Facebook business or fan pages you have on the posting schedule, then I highly recommend it. Getting yourself out there increases your brand awareness and your awareness in general.

The real value in Facebook is the ability to glean personal information about people that you can later use to get them on your side and lead to an easy sale that requires no sleazy closes to make it happen.

For example, I did a Facebook webinar live and tried this experiment on myself. I said, "Let's see how much personal information I can obtain about myself, through the eyes of a stranger, by studying my Facebook posts."

We learned:

- I live in Dallas, Texas.
- I have a Great Dane.
- I have a cat.
- What my favorite restaurants are.
- What sports team I like (and hate).
- Where I'm from.
- What my hobbies are.
- I'm part of Amateur Radio Emergency Services.
- I'm a member of Dallas Community Emergency Response Team.
- I'm an NRA Life Member and Golden Eagle.
- I'm a TSRA (Texas State Rifle Assn.) Life Member.
- I supported Ted Cruz for president in 2016.
- I voted for neither Trump nor Hillary.
- Who some of my old girlfriends are (I know which ones are safe to accept friend requests from, which are the ones my wife has met and become friends with!).
- What my kids' names are.
- How old my kids are.
- Where my kids go to school.
- What kind of car I drive.
- What practically every room of my house looks like.
- What my office looks like (and the location if a savvy Dallasite studies the view out the window).
- Many of the guns I own.
- The fact that I always carry a gun.
- That I gave up alcohol as a self-improvement project (don't worry, I'm not an alcoholic in recovery).

I literally could go on, but I'd bore you, and you get the idea.

This can be done just as easily with Twitter, perhaps even more quickly. People tend to be more opinionated on Twitter so you can figure out their leanings more quickly. As you can see from my example, I obviously lean Republican/Libertarian. Granted, this turns off the portion of my fan base who are Democrats, but that's fine since the Republicans learn this about me and wind up becoming extremely loyal, raving fans, and huge buyers of anything I introduce into the marketplace.

SPEAKING TO ATTAIN PROMINENCE

Speaking is a wonderful thing, because it creates a special dynamic between you and your audience that is difficult to replicate elsewhere.

For example, when I'm on a seminar or convention stage speaking, I use that as a real-life example to explain this dynamic. I point out the fact that I'm not especially tall and at 5 feet 8 inches I'm actually below average height, but when I'm on that stage, I'm the biggest person in the room. I'm a giant. I don't care if half the audience is 6 feet 9 inches tall. It doesn't matter. Being on stage makes me the leader, the boss, the authority figure that everyone will now look up to as a leader.

I used to say, "Even if Donald Trump were in the room, I'd still be the leader and the authority figure." I can't use that example anymore because the president of the United States automatically has the highest social status anywhere in the United States and possibly the entire world. Whenever I run into George W. Bush, who lives nearby, he's very down-to-earth, kind, generous with his time, and easy to talk to. However, that power dynamic is always there. He's a former US president and that gives him automatic authority in any situation. The presence of the Secret Service detail certainly helps too! (I do find it boring that they merely call him "principal" on radio now, instead of whatever cool code name he had while in office. But they all know me so when I walk right up to the prez, they let me; few people can do that.)

Here's a great example of a true story that happened to me. The first time I spoke on a very large stage, it was a three-day seminar, from Friday through Sunday, and I wasn't on until Sunday morning. As the quintessential perpetual student, I of course sat in the audience those first two days learning a lot and taking lots of notes from other speakers. I also made a lot of friends, both in the seminar room and especially at night. That's why, when an event happens locally, I skip it. All the real networking and connecting takes place late at night when everyone is up late mingling, and hey, most of us entrepreneurs are night owls so that's our prime time!

(TIP: If you're a night owl and want to do more, check out my book *The Morning Myth: How Every Night Owl Can Become More Productive, Successful, Happier, and Healthier* [Wiley, 2019]). I've been a night owl all my life and that book explains how I use it to my advantage, not as a handicap, to achieve tremendous success and maximize my productivity while still having huge amounts of free time for family and hobbies.)

After I spoke, however, those "friends" changed. They approached me more cautiously and didn't talk to me like a friend would; instead, they talked to me as if I were an authority figure. (Indeed, I was, as a result of having spoken before the audience.)

What happened is that the entire dynamic had changed. That stage made me the biggest person in the room, and that's how I was treated from that point forward. Those same people who were mingling with me and talking shop at the bar suddenly began supplicating and acting like, well, a typical salesperson who doesn't implement Sales Badassery principles.

And I wasn't a best-selling author yet at the time, so that's not why they looked up to me.

You can do it too. It doesn't take titles or best-selling books or anything else other than your own willingness and drive and *desire* to do it. So be a badass and just do it.

How to Get Started Speaking, Fast

The possibilities of what you can get from public speaking are so limitless that it's something I don't recommend you waste time or procrastinate on doing.

If you've never spoken publicly or are overly nervous about it, that's fine because that's normal human nature. Get a good book or two and learn. Audiobooks may be better in this case.

Then join Toastmaster. In fact, do it now. Then get on Amazon and get the public speaking books. You can read all you want but nothing is going to get you speaking like a true confident pro unless you actually do it.

Two years ago I brought in an intern with the possibility of doing a video show together (video podcast, or vodcast as it's called). Part of why I chose her, and I was up-front about this, is that sex sells. I know someone who has a mediocre podcast going, but he chose a very attractive female cohost, who, despite not being entirely qualified to speak on the topic, attracts enough male viewers that the show is a huge success.

The other reason I chose her is that she was brilliant at sales and business in general. She was a marketing whiz. And, most importantly, she was a dedicated member of her Toastmasters club!

Having someone who can speak sold me on her. Plenty of people responded to my ad, including many equally attractive models, but none had real-world business experience like hers, and being able to speak means being able to go out to Rotary Clubs and the like to speak and promote my business, so that was a no-brainer.

(In case you're wondering, she didn't last because shortly after finding her, my ankle collapsed and I had to go in for the total ankle replacement. Understandably she had to leave to find other income while I was laid up and out of commission.)

Put together a presentation. Keep it to twenty minutes, because that's all you get at Rotary and other similar groups. Indeed this may be a relief to you if you're new to speaking and can't easily take a stage for ninety minutes as I frequently do! I'm not bragging about that, just pointing out that I have a lot in my brain and love to talk about it. After all, that's where this book came from—me spilling out the info that's stored in my brain!

As for slides or a PowerPoint, don't make that the focus of your presentation. What I do is put broad bullet-points on slides, and use that as my guide, or my "notes." Using paper notes is not my preference because it would force me to look down at a podium to access them, and if there's one thing I hate on stage, it's a podium. I like to move around. I get animated when I speak. (Hint: Move around and don't stand lifeless at a podium unless it's a rare venue where you have to—I've been there.)

Now comes the fun part. Of all the service clubs that are open to speakers, the Rotary Club is the best venue in my opinion because they generally contain more business owners and community leaders, along with very wealthy individuals, than any other service club.

Find out what Rotary district you happen to be in, go to the district page on the main Rotary site, and drill down to all the clubs in your area. There are 67 individual Rotary Clubs in Dallas–Fort Worth alone so believe me, you won't have trouble finding quite a few even in a small city.

Go to each club's site and find the program director. This is the person who finds and schedules speakers, so that's whom you want to contact. If there's no program director listed, go directly to the club president and make your pitch to him or her.

Here's the catch with Rotary: There is no selling allowed. *None.* You're there to talk about industry trends (the most engaging topic), specific business problems, talk about the markets if you're in finance, or even speak about volunteer work you do—I've offered to speak about my experiences as a member of the Dallas Community Emergency Response Team along with my service in Amateur Radio Emergency Services.

Although your topic should preferably be closely related to what you have to offer, in order to get people interested in it, speaking about anything will create that dynamic that you're the leader and people will look up to you. At the end of the meeting you'll get people lining up to meet you and exchange business cards. You will make tons of extremely valuable contacts (which will be covered in the next chapter), and those will turn into lucrative sales opportunities for you.

Other groups naturally include chambers of commerce, though with most you have to be a member in order to speak, which is why I stick with small, regional chambers such as the North Dallas Chamber of Commerce. Big, disconnected groups, such as the city's main chamber, tend to be massive and too large to be at all intimate or to give you the chance to get some new business. I have spoken at those groups; however, the smaller ones are far more valuable. I've gained business at them and I've even become the customer of others I've met there. Remember, it's easier to be a big fish in a small pond than a small fish in a big pond who never gets noticed, or worse, gets eaten alive.

Don't stop at Rotary clubs and chambers. The possibilities are endless. As you continue to speak, you'll find opportunities coming your way.

Here's a true story: One day I had a meeting that was postponed, and being in one of my finest suits, I decided that it shouldn't go to waste. It was 11:00 a.m. and I decided to get on Meetup and find a lunch group to go to. The one I chose was less than five minutes from my office so I went.

When I made my introduction I mentioned that I speak regularly on several topics. That takes five seconds to say, if that, so add it to your "thirty-second speech."

After the luncheon adjourned, two different people walked up to me to invite me to speak at two different chambers of commerce, and a third had a lead for me. A fourth became my go-to person for custom shirts! So by choosing *to do something* and *choosing to stay active* rather than just stay in my office plugging away, in a business suit no less, I gained a wealth of opportunity in under an hour by merely mentioning that I speak.

The lesson here is always to be out amongst people. Don't be a loner. Don't spend your time only with sales prospects and customers. The more you get out and meet new people—especially when you can take the platform and leadership role and get people coming to you—the more you'll experience new levels of prosperity you've never even dreamed of.

Sales Badassery Truth

It doesn't matter who you know. What matters is who knows you, and the Sales Badass makes it a top priority to become prominent, respected, and an authority figure in the community.

12

NETWORKING THE SALES BADASSERY WAY

Sales Badasses Don't Network, They Leverage Networking

THE LOSER'S NETWORKING STRATEGY

I used to be a sales loser before I became a Sales Badass. It's okay. Most of us have been. It's all part of the learning process, so I'll describe the loser's networking strategy.

First, they arrive at the networking mixer, pay or show their ticket or whatever, and then mistake number one usually happens: They go to the bar and get a drink.

The reason is to have something in hand, because everyone else has one, but the larger reason is that the sales loser is nervous about talking to strangers and needs some "liquid courage" to get warmed up. The problem is that alcoholic drinks have a tendency to inebriate people and cause cognitive impairment, which alone can kill any chances of making solid, powerful connections. That's why I keep hammering home the point that you must not drink at these functions. Save that for another time.

He'll bounce from group to group and try to introduce himself and make small talk. More often than not he'll be in a group yet not be in the conversation, but rather just observing and listening because he can't get a word in.

Finally he ends up finding some friendly fellow sales reps and hangs out with them. They'll complain about the usual stuff, talk about how they never make any good connections at these events, how they're full of salespeople also wanting to sell something, and spend the evening like they would at any other bar. They enjoy the food and have a few drinks and have a good time.

The problem is that the sales loser walks out empty-handed, or worse, he foolishly gives his business card out to MLMers and financial planners and life insurance agents and many others who will barrage him with dozens of phone calls trying to recruit him into their MLM or otherwise sell him something. (I have nothing against people in those professions, and am friends with many, as long as they're not harassing me to death with cold calls.)

Then for the next week, his sales are impaired because he's afraid to answer the phone. What if it's another one of those obnoxious salesmen he gave his number to? (See how annoying cold calling is when you're on the receiving end?)

In the end, the event was a waste of time and money, and the salesperson is back to square one the next day.

The story I just told you is true. That sales loser was yours truly. I can't tell you how many times I've wasted my time going through that experience. And when I say wasted time, I mean I might as well just have stayed back and made cold calls on the phone because that's about how much in terms of results I got out of those events.

Eventually I realized all they were good for was meeting women, and, being single at the time, I continued going but only for that purpose. They proved useless for getting sales. (C'mon, dressed to the nines like I do, it was like shooting fish in a barrel!)

HOW ONE MAN BECAME "MAYOR" OF HIS CITY

A prominent friend of mine, another author whose name you almost certainly know, got divorced at one point and wanted a fresh start.

He moved to a new city in a new state where he knew no one. And yet he was in the sales game like you are so he realized that networking was his ticket.

Here's what he did: He planned on going to at least three networking groups each and every weekday: A breakfast group, a lunch group, and a happy hour group. (No booze and all business.)

Then he found out where the players in his city hung out, and started going to that bar at night to mingle. With no alcohol flowing through his bloodstream, and some flowing through those of the high-power CEOs and others who hung out there, he easily had the advantage.

In a relatively short period of time he earned the nickname of "mayor" of his city. The one time I happened to be there, we made plans to meet up and spent half a day with him showing me around town, and we couldn't go anywhere—anywhere—without people coming up and saying hi to him.

There were no less than a dozen when we met at Starbucks at 7:45 a.m. when the place was jammed. (Not my time of day!)

The result? He never had to prospect for sales, ever again! He just knew everyone, and everyone knew and liked him. (Remember the Likeability Formula from Chapter 1? Learn it and use it!)

Likewise, when I moved to Dallas in 2012, it was the first time that my wife and I had moved to a new city without knowing a single solitary person.

She made friends fast through our neighborhood's early childhood association, became very involved, and even became president of it for a year. Then once our kids were in school she made tons of friends with fellow moms, as I did with fellow dads.

But I digress. There was no early childhood association for dads, so I was on my own when it came to meeting people, and I chose my friend's strategy, minus the breakfast groups. For starters I'm a night owl and getting up at an insane hour when it's still dark out doesn't work for me. Truth be told, I did try a few, and they were the worst of the bunch. Everyone at those groups was groggy as hell and we'd progress around the room, everyone did his or her 30-second pitch, and then said, "I don't have any leads to share this week." What a joke.

For that reason I stuck with lunch groups, which was tricky for me because most require you to buy lunch—that's why restaurants provide the private rooms for free—and I normally don't eat lunch. I guess I looked like a cheapo buying the smallest thing on the menu, but so what. I made connections. And as I said, I got invitations to speak, to meet with decision-makers, to network with noncompetitors who were in the same space, and so on.

Pretty soon, say, after about three weeks of this, I started running into people I knew everywhere. All over Dallas. I didn't become the unofficial mayor as my friend did but I became extremely well connected. Then, when I joined the Rotary Club of Dallas I met CEOs, generals, owners of large private businesses, community and government leaders, judges… you name it, they were there. (Judges are fantastic people to have as friends. I'm just saying.)

Here's a hint: I highly recommend Rotary. However, of the 67 clubs in my area, there are only two where the players are. So do your research. Look for the club with the largest membership and preferably one that meets in your city's central business district, because the CEOs are sitting on the top floor of those tall buildings and they tend to join the nearest club. Once you're in Rotary for some time and have gotten on a committee or two and done some volunteer work—don't worry, it's not hard or overwhelming—then you can start talking business. Although promoting yourself or your business from the stage is strictly prohibited at Rotary, as a member you're free to network, ask for introductions, get meetings with the players in the club, and more. Perhaps the best part is that as a member, you can go to any Rotary Club meeting anywhere in the world. So make it a point to not just attend your meetings, but to visit with other clubs as well. That's a better option than showing up at a random networking group at lunchtime every day. Go to a Rotary Club instead and be sure to exchange lots of business cards with the people there. And have your introduction down pat! I don't like the term *elevator speech*—thirty seconds as a limit is stupid in my opinion, and it doesn't let you be your genuine self. Talk to people, get to know them personally, and ask them about their kids and other things they love, not just business.

And don't get the wrong impression about Rotary Clubs. I know we all picture our grandfathers there. I got that idea about Rotary during my first summer job as a kid, when I worked at an insurance agency and the two owners were much older men and were very much dedicated to their Rotary Club. The truth is that the larger clubs are extremely diverse, and in fact, my club's largest demographic for new members last year was women in their thirties. Rotary isn't your grandfather's club anymore!

The other "club" you want to check out is a smaller, regional chamber close to you. The North Dallas Chamber of Commerce only costs me $300/year and it's well worth it. Visit as a guest, however, before joining. You want to make sure it's a worthwhile organization before spending your money.

Sales Badassery Tip: Every time you meet someone you want to connect with or otherwise meet with, take a selfie with that person, and then later on or the next day, shoot that person an email with the photo attached so they remember you. It's powerful! You can also use the photo in their contact profile on your smartphone so you remember who you're talking to when they call you. See how that works both ways?

ZERO TO $20,000 A MONTH THROUGH
NETWORKING BADASSERY

Remember when I told you I started a digital marketing agency, and pretty soon I was taking home—netting—$20,000 each and every month with very little work on my part?

That was because of Networking Badassery.

When I started that business, it was a whole new ballgame for me. Up until that time my business activities had been restricted to the Internet, along with any opportunities such as speaking or sales training that came via our website; again, it was all online. Now I was in a local business and in need of local clients, so I had to come up with a strategy to find them and get them on board as paying customers.

I didn't quite know what to do when it was time to get some clients so I started going to networking events. And I mean *a lot* of networking events. I also made a point to invite my technical guy who I outsourced the actual work. He lived quite a drive away on the other side of the Dallas–Fort Worth Metroplex but made as many events as he could, because he was valuable to have around to answer technical questions from prospective clients.

Since I had created a digital marketing agency, which means a business that manages Google AdWords and other online advertising and marketing platforms for clients, I knew I had to differentiate because the space was highly competitive, and is even more so today.

Now at most events, what happens is that everyone does his or her 30-second pitch, going around the room, then someone gets to do a quick 10-minute presentation if it's their turn that week, and that's it. Everyone wraps up and goes back to work and nothing actually turns into results.

Remember the Reality Factor from Chapter 8? The Reality Factor says that fighting reality is painful and will not get results, and that you need to *adapt to reality* and make it work for you.

So there I was, trying to adapt to a world of 30-second pitches when I was used to marketing online and doing two-hour webinars and all that. And here's what I came up with:

"My name is Frank Rumbauskas, owner of ROI Media, and what we do is very simple: We turn your website into a printing press for money."

That's more like a 10-second speech, if that. And it worked.

At every event, multiple people would inevitably come up to me at the end and say, "I'm interested in that making money thing you said about our website!" BOOM—new client! Done!

However, I knew I had to think bigger. The Sales Badass always thinks BIG.

That's when I remembered the importance of leverage. It's the foundation of the Never Cold Call Again® sales philosophy—and I decided to employ leverage in my networking efforts.

Leverage in Networking

It all started off when I realized that I was thinking too small and too local. To counter that, I recorded a series of informational webinars on Google AdWords, with no sales pitch or call to action. They were strictly instructional and informational, and of course my name and contact information were prominently displayed at the bottom of every slide and on the full screen when the presentations ended. On top of that, they were accessible to anyone, anywhere in the world with an Internet connection. I landed clients as far away as Dubai. (He's the person from whom I learned that Qatar is pronounced as *guitar* as I was taught as a kid, not *gutter*, the way news anchors say it. I know this because we ran his ads in Qatar along with several other Middle Eastern countries.)

Not even a month after I uploaded those to YouTube (remember the power of that?) and then embedded those videos in my LinkedIn profile, I received a phone call one morning from a panicked owner of an advertising agency, saying that he just had a client ask for Google AdWords services. And he wanted them now.

Next thing I knew, I was on a conference call with the ad agency's rep along with the owner, and of course the client. I was introduced as a member of their team and I sold and closed the client on a Google AdWords management plan right then and there.

The owner was on cloud nine and asked if they could take me to lunch that day, wherever I chose in Dallas, even though they were in the suburbs, about 45 minutes away.

We met for lunch at a restaurant I like about 10 minutes from my office. After all the talk and questions about how I can handle the traffic and congestion in Dallas rather than move out to where it's quiet and cheaper (that would bore me to death), we started talking business and the owner repeatedly told me how thrilled he is and that he wants this to be an ongoing relationship with me and my people—all outsourced but personally trained by me—to keep this going.

We also met again, privately in his office, and put together our informal plan for how we would work together.

This resulted in a very lucrative business relationship that brought me lots and lots of clients, and I had a lot of fun driving out there on a regular basis and working with the team at that agency.

And that's when the light bulb went on: It occurred to me that I was employing *leverage* in this situation. I had connected with one person who was bringing me multiple new clients.

You can guess what I did next. I sent direct mail letters out to every smaller ad agency that I knew probably wouldn't have in-house AdWords people, then followed up with phone calls and requested meetings.

It wasn't long before I had multiple agencies I was providing services to, and that resulted in a lot of business—I mean a lot!

All because of using leverage by networking not with people who could buy from me once, but with people who could send me a continuous, consistent, ongoing stream of new clients, I was pocketing over $20,000 a month in under a year.

I also used leverage in networking 20 years ago when I was a 20-something, young and hungry sales professional. That's why I had a referral agreement in place with a group of complementary, noncompetitive salespeople.

Since I was selling AT&T business telephone systems (which became Lucent Technologies during the time I was working there), I cruised on over to the AT&T services office, which provided the actual phone lines, Internet connections, and so on, that the phone systems plugged into.

Now, we did have a company referral plan, but it was lousy. No one was going to go out of their way to refer someone for 20 bucks. I approached our regional manager to discuss this and he agreed to increase the payouts. Victory! I made it even more tempting for them by increasing those numbers with cash out of my commissions. After all, I was getting freebie sales that took no effort on my part to obtain, so it only made sense to share a quarter of my commission with the referring person.

Initially they would send me leads and I'd pursue them. After some time, we agreed to set up a lunch meeting once they had someone who they knew needed equipment. They would buy the customer lunch, introduce me, and we would explain together why they needed my solution (which they already needed). Then I'd walk out with a signed check and contract.

It was really that easy.

The rest of the reps in the office started rumors that I was the sales manager's favorite and that he was giving me all the leads that came in, or that I was getting all the call-in leads, and even that I was stealing leads from others! (Ironically, I'd had leads stolen from me, which is why I then started working from home so they had no idea what I was up to or who I was working.)

MY FAVORITE NETWORKING VENUE

The best networking venues of all to me, besides LinkedIn, are private, invitation-only business roundtable groups.

I used to belong to one called Dallas Business Alliance. In spite of having to get up two hours early to get to the 7:30 a.m. meetings every Wednesday, I was there each and every week. The group consisted of CEOs, thought leaders like myself, higher-ups in companies, corporate/business law attorneys, and more.

The nice thing about the group is that while the meetings were about general business topics, with one person—either a member or guest—presenting that week, we followed a plan whereby each member would meet one-on-one with another member until we covered them all; then we would start all over again.

That's where the networking happened. The specific purpose of these one-on-one private meetings outside of the group was to determine what type of people we'd like referred to us. Then we'd explain that to each member individually, listen to their needs in return, and take notes so we could mentally scan our contact list and think of who might be a good prospect.

You'll have to network and get involved to get invited to this type of group. They exist everywhere, and in fact now that Dallas Business Alliance disbanded because almost no one liked the too-early meeting times and attendance dwindled over time, I'm planning on starting one with someone I met while speaking at a local chamber group. (See the power of speaking?)

Side note: You don't have to be a morning person to be successful. That's why I wrote an entire book on why night owls are, overall, more successful than morning larks and can continue to become even more successful. It all started when a colleague put out a research paper—really a promotional piece—claiming that the most common trait among the extremely successful is that they are early risers.

I immediately called bullshit on this and did my own research. I learned that night owls actually earn more money in a lifetime, on average, than morning larks. But the big eye-opener is that, in my own research, the most common trait among the highly successful is that they don't drink alcohol.

Now I'm not saying you have to quit drinking (unless of course it's a problem, in which case you absolutely should). What I am saying is that, unless you're a natural early riser, there's no need to drag yourself out of bed to get to a 7:00 or 7:30 a.m. networking group. You'd be far better off getting your needed rest than going to an event where you're not fully awake, then have a less-than-productive rest of your day because you're half asleep the entire time.

Sales Badassery Truth

The Sales Badass will engage in one-on-one networking when it is lucrative; however, the Sales Badass knows that working exponentially will always outperform working linearly. As a result, the Sales Badass looks for leveraged networking connections, such as my advertising agency owner, who can send a steady and consistent stream of hot leads, not just one-offs here and there.

13

SALES BADASSES THINK *BIG*!

I can't stop thinking big, I can't stop thinking big!
—*"Caravan" by Rush (Written by Lee/Lifeson/Peart)*

YOUR RESULTS WILL NEVER EXCEED YOUR THOUGHTS

Thoughts are things. —Napoleon Hill

You will become what you think about. —Earl Nightingale

Write down your goal on a piece of paper. —Napoleon Hill

There are probably hundreds, if not thousands, of quotes similar to these, all the way back to the ancient philosophers of thousands of years ago.

It's amazing how times never change, isn't it?

For all the war and human loss and upheaval and economic uncertainty and everything else we hear in the news, when I sit down to read an old book, say *The Law of Success* by Napoleon Hill, originally published in 1925, I'm astonished to see the author talking about the very same problems the world faces today, then he goes on to say that people have been worrying about the same things down through the centuries.

It's true! And it goes back to what I said about one of the very basic blocks of sales professionalism: *Human nature never changes.* That's why people always worry about the same things, regardless of what century or millennia it happens to be. Likewise, it's why all sales techniques work across all industries, and why many ideas you can pick up from books written a century ago will still work today. Human nature doesn't change, and sales are sales.

So, with that in mind, let's say you've mastered all there is to know about sales, and you've proven in practice that you not only talk the talk, but that you walk the walk and can produce sales.

Assuming you've got the skillset down and you can execute it, the only remaining obstacle in your way is your mindset.

Are you thinking big? Or are you doing what most people do—worrying about next month's bills, where the next sales will come from, setting targets in your mind (such as your monthly quota) that are way too low, and so on?

Because if you don't think big, and by big I mean *huge*, you simply won't get the sales results you are capable of by allowing your mindset to limit you. Nor will you achieve success in life in general.

THE ASS-BACKWARDS SALES-GOAL-SETTING METHOD

First of all, forget the "sales-training goal-setting method."

That method states that cold calls equal appointments equal sales, but that's not true anymore. All sales managers are guilty of teaching it, believing it, and using it. "Increase your activity and increase your income" are the mantra. We're told to do the sales math to "motivate" ourselves. Have you heard this one? (I'll bet you have.) "If you make 500 dollars' commission per sale and it takes five appointments to get the sale and 20 cold calls to get one appointment, then each cold call is worth five dollars in your pocket."

Did anyone ever really believe this crap?

Hey boss, put your money where your mouth is! If that were really true companies would simply pay you five dollars for each call made. But they don't. That's because that equation never works out in the real world—not for anyone. The simple fact is that you are only paid for completed sales. Directing salespeople to make more calls and increase activity is a weak excuse for a sales manager or trainer to justify his or her job. Cold calling is an expensive waste of your time. The reasons companies have you cold calling is because it wastes your time and money, not theirs. You only make money when you close a sale, and yet over 80% of most salespeople's time is spent looking for someone to sell to.

The bottom line is that salespeople cannot afford to continue fooling away time on low-result activities like cold calling. It's a way for companies to save money at your expense. You must focus your attention on activities that get real results in this new Information Age economy and the effectiveness of cold calling fell dramatically when we left the old Industrial Age and entered into this new Information Age.

Self-marketing is the key to success in today's selling environment and is the "secret" of all those top producers who obviously don't cold call and won't tell you what it is they're doing to make those huge numbers each and every month. Remember, Napoleon Hill's most popular book is called *Think and Grow Rich,* not *Cold Call and Stay Poor.* Don't become a victim of this ass-backwards sales training activity-planning model. It is *not* big-thinking goal setting. It's a loser's strategy that will set you up for failure.

HOW TO TRAIN YOUR MIND TO PRODUCE BIG

That "method" I just outlined is what all but one or two sales managers I'd ever worked for would push on the sales team. It's ridiculous. Don't ever buy into it, because it never works out. For anyone. Ever.

I personally follow a modified version of Napoleon Hill's goal setting methodology to get whatever you want.

Now keep in mind that writing down your goals isn't enough. You need to implement and execute and understand that it takes work to succeed, regardless of what you're trying to accomplish.

What Hill said to do is to write down the amount of money you desire, name a timeframe (a deadline) for its acquisition, state what you intend to give in return for the money you desire, then carry out your plan with persistence until you reach your goal while reading your statement of desire aloud, immediately upon waking in the morning, and as the last thing you do before going to bed at night. (Yes, I know there are other pleasant things you can do in bed besides sleep, so literally make that the last thing you do before going to sleep.)

I've found some problems with this. The first is that it tells you to come up with a number and write it down. I can tell you from both my personal experience, along with that of those I've worked with, that people rarely achieve the goal they write down. Something always happens, or something comes up, or a slew of expected deals fall through, and they never hit the number.

The second problem for me is the idea of having one goal. I don't have one goal or dream. I have lots of dreams! And they're big! So it's okay to write down multiple things you want to achieve.

Here's the methodology I use:

1. Come up with a specific number; it's important to be specific. Just like setting a sales appointment for 3:00 p.m. doesn't have the same impact and urgency as setting it for, say, 3:12 p.m., your goal needs to be specific, so put some thought into it and don't just pull a number out of your head.

   Then double it. If you hit that goal, double it again.

I say double it because, again, no one ever hits his or her goal as originally stated. By doubling that goal, you set yourself up for falling short of the doubled number, but you will exceed your original goal. Genius!

A good and reliable method to set your number, if it's directly related to sales goals, is to double your quota. If your plan is to actually bring in 200%, then make your goal 300%. You get the idea.

Then, don't stop there. Think *big*. What could you do if you knew you could do anything? What dreams did you have as a kid that you gave up on? (I know plenty of people who changed careers midlife when they found themselves discontented with their current success and chose to pursue the dreams they *always* really wanted.)

If you want a private jet, write it down. However, first get online and do some research on private jets. Look up specifications and ranges and things like that. Come up with one specific make and model and let that be your goal. The more specific you can be in setting goals, the higher your chances of attaining them.

Want a new Bentley? Maserati? That S-Class Mercedes-Benz that motivated me to start my business and be in the position I am in today? Write them down, but have the specific make and model in mind, right down to the color, wheels, and other options.

When I set my sights on that car, I went to the dealer and sat in one for some time. I took it all in. I memorized the interior and burned it into my mind. I remembered the aroma of the leather (it was on my shirt later that evening when I took it off). Then, whenever I was driving the car I had at the time, I would replace the view from the driver's seat with the inside of that big Benz. Then, as if by a stroke of magic, I had it in less than a year. (This is powerful stuff, so use it wisely.)

2. Here's the point at which I disconnect from Hill's method. Don't write down just one goal if you have more than one; write them all down!

Hill says you must have one definite chief aim at any given time. It can be a lifetime goal, like how Bill Clinton wanted to be president since he was a kid, or it can be a short-term goal such as making X number of dollars within one year.

Personally, I can never come up with just one thing to write down. I have a lot of goals. I'm out to create the world's premier sales consulting firm. I'm working to become a thought leader in other areas of success besides just sales. Being a great dad and husband, so I can keep my fantastic relationship with my wife and kids alive, is one of my goals.

3. Create a timeline for the acquisition of your goals. In other words, set a definite deadline, because without one, you'll never reach them. (Notice that I don't use the word *dream* here, because once a dream has been put into writing, it has become a goal.) Make your deadline realistic but not so far out that it's easy for you. After all, you want what you want sooner rather than later. The importance of this is because without a deadline, you'll fall into the human nature trap of procrastination—putting off until tomorrow what should have been done yesterday or last month or last year. Procrastination is an inborn trait that all humans are cursed with, so by writing down the date by which you'll achieve your goals, you ensure that you don't procrastinate and will stick to your guns. Likewise, feeding that deadline to your subconscious mind will help it to make sure it does its job in time. Speaking of the subconscious...

4. Make your goals real in your own mind and bring them to life in your imagination. As you read them every morning and night, see and feel and believe yourself in possession of the goal if it's a material thing, like I did with that car, or if it's an intangible, imagine yourself in achievement of it. And I mean really

concentrate—burn those images into your mind. Picture that money so close to you, you can smell it and touch it. Don't drive your own car. Use it, but when you're in it, always imagine you're in the car of your dreams, because that's how you'll get it. The idea is to always picture yourself in achievement and/ or in possession of your goals. It's very similar to the "mental movies" I described in Chapter 4. Use those too! By doing this, you manage to get the ideas past the "gatekeeper" of your sub-conscious mind. It's the subconscious that does all the heavy lifting and that will give you the plans and ways and means of getting what you want in the real world. More on that later.

5. Your money-making plan. This is where I disconnect from Hill's methodology. When I decided I wanted that car, I had no idea whatsoever about how I'd get it. It was shortly after 9/11 and the event had dramatically impacted my income when the entire economy came to a screeching halt for what seemed like forever. I was fighting to make the payments on my current car, and yet I still wanted, with a burning desire, to have that six-figure Mercedes-Benz sitting in my garage!

All I did was live, eat, sleep, breathe, and imagine myself in it day and night. After several months of this, *Never Cold Call Again*® was born from an idea that seemingly came out of nowhere, and less than a year later, I was in my new car. Without any loan or debt, either.

So don't worry too much about what you plan to give in return for your goals. When it comes to making the sales number you set as your target, that's easy; you're providing your services to your employer or to your own business in the capacity of a sales professional and you also provide outstanding service to your customers.

With the others, however, it's more intangible, as that car was for me.

THE DEATH KNELL OF GOAL ACHIEVEMENT

Setting large, ambitious goals can be daunting at first. And this is the single largest roadblock to your success, meaning if you write a big goal such as buying a private jet, do not—and I mean *do not*—start letting your mind wander and begin wondering how on earth you're going to get it.

Now it's time for me to fess up: I didn't just want that car. I had a twofold goal of having the car and being financially free of a job.

I had absolutely no idea how on earth I was going to do that! After all, it was hard enough to get a good job in the immediate aftermath of 9/11, let alone figuring out how to start a business that would allow me not only to be free of a job but also to afford that car without making much of a dent in my bank account.

And if I had tried to figure out how I was going to get it, I would have failed!

You see, what happens when you settle on a goal and then focus on that goal, see it, feel it, and imagine it already in your possession, your subconscious mind takes it over and runs with it.

As you go through your day and while you sleep at night, your subconscious mind is constantly at work. However, the subconscious is like a rich, fertile garden spot. If you don't keep that garden full of valuable crops, it will soon be overrun with weeds! Likewise, if you don't keep your own mind filled with positive thoughts and goals and ideas, the weeds—negative thoughts, fear, and anxiety—will take over and leave no room for the positive.

When I fixated on the dual goals of being free of a job and driving that S500, I fixated only on having those things, *not trying to figure out how I'd get them.*

Correction: I did make the mistake once of figuring out how I'd get them and whatever absurd plan I'd come up with said I'd be free of a job at age 55. Heck, that was retirement age when I was a kid! In reality, I achieved it at age 30.

The reason I achieved it so quickly and seemingly with ease was because I never let myself dwell on how I'd possibly achieve those goals. Instead, I continually fed them to my subconscious mind.

Then one day, after about a year of this, I was at home, in front of my computer, and the idea popped into my head to create a course detailing the exact methodology that I used to generate leads without cold calling. (By that point I was doing very well in sales and hadn't made a cold call in years.)

I named it *Cold Calling Is a Waste of Time: Sales Success in the Information Age.* I used one of those online website-builder tools that took less than half an hour, put the site online, deposited my five dollars to Google AdWords to get some ads up, and I had my first sale 30 minutes later.

The rest, as they say, is history. I was free of the job and nine months later I walked into the Mercedes-Benz dealer to go get my dream car.

The way I quit my last job ever is a great story in itself: I did it *Office Space* style, as in the movie. I simply stopped showing up. At a big corporation like that, it literally took three weeks for anyone to notice I hadn't been around and to get a call from the boss asking if I still worked there! Seriously, if you work for a big dumb company and the day comes to begin your life of freedom, try it. It'll be one of the funniest things you ever do.

GOALS TURNED OBSESSIONS

After you practice this long enough, your goals will take on a life of their own and become all-consuming obsessions for you. They will become all you think about, day and night. You'll have dreams about your goals.

As Dr. Hill wrote, having a dream won't cut it; you must reduce that dream to writing, which converts it into a goal, and, most importantly, is the first step to making that goal a physical reality. Because once the goal is on paper, it is indeed something physical, and then you're on your way.

More importantly, however, is the fact that as you read and see and feel your goals in your possession twice daily—more often if possible—they stop being goals and they become all-consuming obsessions! And once you have an all-consuming obsession, you have something that's now within your grasp and that you can actually attain within your chosen timeframe.

You'll stop wasting time on efforts and activities that don't bring you closer to your goals. Your mind will direct you away from them. Bad habits that held you down in the past will begin to disappear with little or no effort on your part. When I decided to give up alcohol as a self-improvement experiment, I didn't just declare one day, "I *quit!*" I let the idea that the most successful people don't drink dwell in my mind, which in turn made me lose the desire to drink, until one day I noticed that I hadn't had any in a while, and *then* I made the decision to avoid it for good.

You'll find ways and means of obtaining your goals start to appear to you as if by magic. The reality is that they've been there all along; however, until your goals became an all-consuming obsession, you simply didn't notice them. Now your subconscious mind is directing your conscious mind to watch for them and make you take notice.

Opportunities to get to your goals will begin presenting in the form of people, contacts, capital, and more. I don't know exactly how this works—no one does—but I do know that it works. I'm speaking from experience when I say that.

For example, I don't have to understand electricity and the internal workings of a light bulb to flip on a light switch and get light. I just know that it works.

Likewise, rather than being skeptical, or wasting time and money buying endless books about goal setting, be a Sales Badass and *just do it*. Take this information on goals and how to get them, and *do it*.

> ### Sales Badassery Truth
>
> *Sales Badasses don't think big, and they don't waste time. They use effective methods of programming their minds to bring their goals to them on a silver platter, and then implement and execute, which is what brings home results.*

Epilogue

As you can now see, a Sales Badass is not your run-of-the-mill sales professional.

Here's a word of caution: Although you can implement the techniques in this book endlessly, "techniquing" people into buying won't cut it.

The master key to Sales Badassery, the secret, is all in the mindset of a Sales Badass.

Sales Badasses don't take any shit from anyone. If a prospect isn't paying attention or keeps answering the phone during your appointment, you get up, and ask to reschedule when they can give their full attention.

Sales Badasses don't tolerate lateness. Never wait around for a late prospect. They're being disrespectful to you. A Sales Badass will leave and reschedule at a better time.

Like the Mafia, Sales Badasses tolerate no disrespect. Ever. And yet they have a way of making people like them, instantly, and give them their respect. As an example, I remember the infamous mobster John Riggi, capo and subsequently head of the DeCavalcante crime family. He was a friend of the family and lived very near where I grew up in New Jersey. When he would drop by the house when I was a little kid, I don't remember a big bad Mafioso; I remember an extremely nice, likeable man. I never knew about any of that other stuff until later on.

The Sales Badass is *always* the best-dressed person in the room. Always. And the persona matches the outfit.

Sales Badasses never chase and beg. They don't pursue people but, rather, bring enough value—and, more important, power—to the table so the people want to pursue *them.*

The Sales Badass is king of his domain and expects those around him to follow and take his lead. This doesn't mean he's a jerk, but rather that he tolerates no nonsense. If someone wants to hang around his desk and chit-chat, the Sales Badass says he's busy and we'll talk later.

Sales Badasses know where they are going. Their goals are on paper, and they're revisited at least twice daily and become burning obsessions. This guarantees their achievement. When a goal is met, a new and loftier one replaces it.

Sales Badasses are selective about who they let into their network. If they meet someone who cannot be a leveraged source of new business, that person probably doesn't deserve to be in the same social circle as Sales Badasses.

Ultimately, the Sales Badass puts together everything in this book to be the dominant force in every sales interaction. He controls the outcome, not the decision-maker. In fact, done right, Sales Badassery philosophy makes *you* the decision-maker. Because when you follow the rules of being a Sales Badass, every sales interaction naturally leads to a sale, without you having to "sell" and with the prospect happily buying of his own free will.

In that regard, the Sales Badass replaces the negative stereotype of a salesperson with that of a very positive one.

I know this book has given you everything you need to become a Sales Badass. So put it all together ... and begin experiencing life as a true Sales Badass. For more information, visit www.SalesBadassery.com.

Acknowledgments

Every time I sit down to write a book, I think, "Oh, this will be easy. I've done it enough times before."

Inevitably, that is rarely the case. Starting a book is a lot like going to the gym. After a long time off, say for several years after relocating to Dallas, getting back to the gym took forever. As in over a year. That's because no one wants to go to the gym for the first time.

But once I'm in, I transform into a beast. I can't get enough. I have to literally put up a fight with myself to keep from going to the gym too often, which would result in overtraining. (I'm going there as soon as I put this down.)

With a book, it's the same. Once I can get myself to sit down and just do it, it begins to flow. And pretty soon it's like the gym; thoughts will pop into my mind and make me want to drop everything I'm doing and get back to writing, which usually isn't possible. Thankfully I learned a great trick from the great Jeffrey Gitomer: I simply text those ideas to myself. That way they cannot get lost.

It was a thrill to work, once again, with the same one-two team who hand-held me through my first published book and its subsequent follow-ups: Matt Holt and Shannon Vargo at John Wiley & Sons. And just as many thanks go to Kelly Martin, who is now a part of that team (a trio?) and has been tremendously kind and helpful. The crew at Wiley truly are a pleasure to work with, in a world where problems and stress never seem to stop coming at us from all directions. At one time I shopped publishers and thought about making a move, but the people at Wiley are quintessential professionals and so easy to work with that I wisely decided to stay with them. It's like my publishing "home." And they're less than 30 minutes away from where I grew up—what a small world, considering my first book was written while living in Phoenix, Arizona!

I'd like to thank my ankle surgeon, Dr. Carr Vineyard, MD, at the Carrell Clinic in Dallas, Texas, for giving me my life back. I lived in chronic pain for over ten years all thanks to an old running injury and walked like someone twice my age, right down to using a cane toward the end. (Although it made me feel like Dr. Gregory House, which was cool. I even got the same cane with flames on it. "It looks like it's going fast!") Ever since Dr. Vineyard installed a shiny new German-made ankle in my left foot, I get to live pain-free and also free of the impediments that stunted my love of public speaking for a very long time. To him I will be forever grateful, though he'd say he was just doing his job. Thanks also go to Dr. Andrew Gerken, MD, at Newport Beach Orthopedic Institute, who performed a minor surgery way back in 2008 that was beyond successful and lasted double the amount of time of its prognosis, which was only five years tops, and his operation is what allowed me to get a new ankle in the first place. He's another who'd say he was just doing his job.

If I had not been able to heal and get on with my life, this book might very well not have happened.

Speaking of true heroes who will also claim, "I was just doing my job," I can never give enough respect and gratitude to the men and women of our Armed Forces and those of armed forces throughout the free world. This wonderful, free nation that was born in the minds of only 56 men who affixed their signatures to the Declaration of

Independence has been preserved by the spilled blood of America's fighting men and women down through the centuries. I never truly understood their sacrifice until I met my wife and then found myself part of a largely military family. (Police too—that'd be my brother-in-law, bravely patrolling one of the worst parts of New York City on a daily basis.) I sincerely thank every member and every veteran of our armed services and also appreciate the great work being done by so many for the benefit of veterans, such as local resident George W. Bush's ongoing, tireless dedication to helping disabled veterans of war that I see right before my eyes here in Dallas.

Likewise, I never appreciated what our police and firefighters go through until I joined Dallas's CERT (Community Emergency Response Team). Our job is to go in and cover for police, fire, and medical until they arrive, and then to be their force multiplier once they're on scene. The amount of knowledge and skills required to become a CERT is vast, from emergency medical ops to search and rescue to firefighting to you name it. Our emergency personnel do a lot more than put out fires and respond to police calls. Most of what they do is behind the scenes and out of the news media's public eye, and is far more diversified than any of us can imagine. And I'm fortunate to live in a city where the police smile and wave when they see you, the way I remember as a kid. It's largely thanks to them that I'm afforded the safety to comfortably live and work and write these books knowing someone always has my back.

The most important thanks go to my family. First to my parents for bringing me into this world in the first place. Although I may have had my share of fights with them growing up, looking back, I can see now as a parent myself that they tried their hardest and did the best job they possibly could for me. (Pretty good result too, eh?) I'm fortunate to have three living grandparents at my age, which means my kids have three living great-grandparents, something I never got to experience. And as you saw in the dedication, my maternal grandmother, Nannie Bea, has always been like a mother to me. We've enjoyed a special bond since the day I came into this world that will last long after she's passed on into the next world.

My wife, Dana, gets a special thanks, especially for enduring and sticking around for what can be a roller-coaster ride of a serial entrepreneur's life. Her love is never-ending and, on days when I have the kids all to myself and they drive me crazy, I have a very special appreciation for all that she does for our family! She is the most grounded, down-to-earth, and intelligent woman I've ever known and I consider myself blessed and very fortunate to be her husband.

I'd especially like to thank Dana's parents, Patty and Kevin, for bringing *her* into the world. I never understand why anyone complains about seeing their in-laws, because I love mine.

And of course, last but definitely not least—not even remotely— are my two beautiful daughters, Agnes and Maeve. As much as I hate to see you grow up and eventually leave us someday, it has been the most precious experience of my life watching you grow. Most parents wish their kids would stay little forever, but watching you grow and develop is the single greatest thrill I get from life. It's hard for me to believe that I was never sure if I really wanted kids, and yet, if I had to live life all over again without you, I simply wouldn't. You're only five and seven years old, so please enjoy every minute of your childhood naïveté to the fullest. The world will have enough problems waiting for you when you grow up, so let's just play for now. I know I could spend my life living in airplanes and hotel rooms and on endless stages in the name of money, but I'd rather stay home and spend that time with you. For that will be worth far more to you when you're grown up than any amount of money I could possibly give you.

Having said that, you can make your lives anything you want them to be. There will be problems and challenges and defeats along the way. There are lots of them for all of us, but I know that what I'm trying hard to instill into your minds now will help you overcome all that and hopefully make your adulthood just as fun-filled as your childhood is right now. And remember that no matter what happens, your mommy and daddy will be right here, always ready to offer a helping hand, to give our support, and most important of all, to always, always love you unconditionally and for you to know that even when the time comes for you to be grown adults and have to leave us, our door and our hearts will forever be open to you.

May you both grow into Sales Badasses regardless of your career choices, for sales skills are universal life skills. And I'll be damned if I'm not going to give you every possible tool you'll need in order to make your marks on the world. As Journey said, "Only the young can say they're free to fly away." So spread your wings and fly!

About the Author

The late Frank Rumbauskas had a lot of labels: *New York Times* best-selling author, sales guru, top internet marketer, success mentor, Google-Certified AdWords Expert, and many more.

Frank's rise to success began in the in-your-face world of outside sales, where he learned the hard way that chasing prospects and goals only kept them out of reach. While working as an account executive for a Fortune 100 company, Frank did what he was told and chased every prospect. He cold called, he went through the traditional steps of a sale that he was taught, he placed prospects and customers first, and as a result he experienced nothing but failure and frustration.

Then, Frank learned about the science of social dynamics from a star performer and everything changed. This top producer took Frank under his wing, and explained the basics of why people buy, why one person has the power and the next doesn't, and how and why these principles apply in any and all situations, business or otherwise. Frank's sales results more than tripled—almost immediately—as a result of applying these principles.

Frank took these principles, perfected them, built systems around them, and applied them anywhere to get anything.

Frank left the sales profession at the top of his game, and helped others approach their work and lives from a position of power. A serial entrepreneur in industries including internet, telecom, and insurance, Frank experienced explosive growth first-hand without using obsolete tactics that drain profits.

In addition to Frank's best-selling sales and marketing books, he was routinely featured as a top internet marketing expert in seminars, webinars, and more. The reason was simple: while Frank was known as a best-selling author and top entrepreneur, it was his expertise in internet marketing that got him there. Internet marketing was Frank's top passion, and the engine behind his financial freedom.

Frank was frequently quoted in mainstream media including *Entrepreneur*, *Investor's Business Daily*, and *Selling Power*, and his books continue to help sales leaders achieve their full potential.

INDEX

R

Q